RICHARDS'

BICYCLE
REPAIR
MANUAL

BICYCLE
REPAIR
MANUAL

RICHARD BALLANTINE & RICHARD GRANT

DORLING KINDERSLEY
LONDON • NEW YORK • STUTTGART

A DORLING KINDERSLEY BOOK

Editors
Roddy Craig, Lol Henderson

Designer
Sam Grimmer

Production
Louise Daly

Managing Editor
Josephine Buchanan

Managing Art Editor
Lynne Brown

First published in Great Britain in 1994 by Dorling Kindersley Limited
9 Henrietta Street, London WC2E 8PS

Copyright © 1994 Dorling Kindersley Limited, London
Text copyright © 1994 Richard Ballantine & Richard Grant

A CIP catalogue record for this book is available from the British Library

ISBN 07513 0087 X

Commissioned photography by
Philip Gatward and Jane Stockman

Reproduced by Colourscan, Singapore
Printed in Hong Kong

Contents

Introduction

RIDING A BIKE IS FUN, and the better the mechanical condition of the bike, the more fun it is to ride. A bike is a mechanical extension of your body, and you can usually feel when a bike needs attention – the brakes become mushy, or gear shifts take longer. You hear odd sounds – perhaps a sticking freewheel, or the chain catching on a derailleur cage. Service your bike regularly, however, and such problems will rarely arise. Bike maintenance is easy to learn. If you are a novice mechanic, begin with simple tasks such as checking tyre pressure, light lubrication, and adjusting control cables, brake blocks, saddle, handlebars, and control lever positions. In time, go on to more complex jobs such as servicing bearings and the transmission. You'll soon become proficient, and seldom suffer the inconvenience of a breakdown. Of course, jobs such as frame repair and realignment require experience and specialized tools, and are best done by a bike shop. Most bike maintenance, however, you can do yourself. Keeping your bike in tip-top shape is very satisfying – and makes riding even more enjoyable.

Richard Ballantine

Richard Grant

Bicycle Anatomy

SPECIALIZATION HAS LED to different types of bike, from racing bikes to mountain bikes, but basically all bikes are the same, although components vary in design, weight, and ease and method of use. A bike is made up of a frame, wheels, transmission, brakes, stem, handlebars, and saddle. Frames always bear their maker's name, but all other parts are usually supplied by different manufacturers. The precise breakdown of a bike's components is called the specification. Familiarize yourself with bike terminology; it will make repair instructions much easier to follow.

Saddle

Seat post

Micro-adjust seat bolt

Cable guide

Quick-release seat post bolt

Brake bridge

Freewheel sprockets/cogs

Cable anchor bolt

Front derailleur

Derailleur pivot bolt

Cage

Rear derailleur body

Rim

Barrel adjuster

Cable anchor bolt

Spider

Chainring

Cage

Crank dust-cap

Chain

Tension pulley/wheel

Rear gear cable

Cable stop

HYBRID BIKE

The *Canondale* SH600 shown here is a hybrid model that blends the light weight and speed of a sport road bike with the rugged durability and versatility of a mountain bike. Perfect for riding to the office one day and exploring a muddy track the next, hybrid bikes are flexible and enjoyable – great bikes for the all-round cyclist.

Grips

Handlebar

Gear lever/shifter

Headset

Stem bolt

Brake lever

Stem

Rear brake cable housing

Front brake cable

Straddle yoke

Straddle wire

Brake cable anchor bolt

Cantilever brake arm

Brake block

Waterbottle bosses

Brake pivot bolt

Quick-release hub clamp

Tyre wall

Toe strap

Toe clip

Pedal

Crank

Pannier rack mounting boss

Eyelets for mudguards/pannier rack

Hub/spoke flange

Tyre tread

Spoke nipple

Spoke

Hub axle/spindle

Presta valve

Valve cap

The Frame

BICYCLE FRAME DESIGN involves many inter-related elements. Slight variations produce very different characteristics and performance levels. While modern materials and technologies aid the creation of new designs, ultimately the feel and handling of a bike results from the frame-builder's own experimentation and instincts. Frames are made either from refined-ore metals, such as steel, aluminium, and titanium, or from composites of structural fibres, such as carbon, glass, or spectra, with a glue or plastic binder.

TOP TUBE

Mountain bike top tubes often slope from the head tube to the seat tube, strengthening the frame and giving the rider more clearance. Road bike top tubes tend to be more or less horizontal.

Top tube

FRAME GEOMETRY

Mountain bike frames are designed for off-road manoeuvrability and strength. The geometry (comprising the frame angles, chain-stay length, rake, and trail) is relaxed for predictable steering and stability. Road bike frames feature steeper geometry for more responsive handling.

Brake bridge

Merlin titanium mountain bike frame

Seat tube

Brazed-on cantilever brake mounting boss

Seat stays

SEAT TUBE

To allow more movement under the rider when cycling over rough ground, and a low saddle on descents, the seat tube on a mountain bike is 3–5 in shorter than on the rider's road bike frame size.

Bottom bracket

Dropouts

Derailleur hanger

Chain stays

CHAIN-STAY LENGTH

On mountain bikes, chain-stay length varies between 16¾ and 18½ in. Longer stays aid stability. On a racing bike the length is from 40–42 cm. This gives nimble handling but leaves no space for mudguards or wide tyres. Touring bikes have long chain stays to keep the rear pannier weight centred over the rear axle, and to avoid fouling the rider's heels.

BOTTOM BRACKET

The height of a mountain bike frame bottom bracket varies from 29–33 cm (11½–13 in), giving good ground clearance for obstacles. Road bike bottom brackets are usually lower, which reduces wind resistance.

FRAME SET

Bicycle tubing is made in a range of different quality grades and weights, and sold in matched frame sets for building specific bike types. Frame-builders sometimes mix tubes of different types to produce frames finely tuned for the weight and riding style of individual riders.

JOINING TECHNIQUES

Modern alloy steels are versatile and can be TIG-welded by machine or brazed (a process of joining tubes using a non-ferrous alloy such as brass, which has a lower melting point than the metals being joined). Aluminium can also be TIG-welded, or bonded with glue. The finest-quality frames are still joined by hand.

Steerer tube

Head tube

Down tube

WHEELBASE

The wheelbase of a bicycle frame is the distance between the wheel axles, or the points where the tyres contact the ground. Mountain bikes have longer wheelbases than road bikes for greater stability. The short wheelbase and steep geometry of road-racing bikes give them very fast steering reaction.

Brazed-on cantilever brake mounting boss

Forks

Dropouts

WILL THE FRAME BREAK?

Metal breaks either from an impact that exceeds its strength, or due to fatigue induced by repeated small stresses. Steel and titanium have fatigue limits and will not break if the stress is under limits. Aluminium has no fatigue limit, so each stress impact will cause weakening, and eventual failure. Aluminium frame designers acknowledge this, and incorporate enough strength for long-term safety. Even if well worn, a steel or titanium frame will stay almost as good as new, but not aluminium frames, which are thought to have a useful life of three to five years. Steel frames may need to be realigned if the bike has had a real thrashing. Composite frames are still too new to gauge long-term durability, but, as with aluminium, cumulative stress may lead to eventual failure.

FORKS

The forks on mountain bikes have to be extremely strong to endure enormous loads and successive impacts over rough terrain. It is now common to have suspension systems built into the forks for greater rider comfort and steering control. Road bike forks have to endure less shock and so can be made much lighter.

Size and Fit

THE MOST IMPORTANT feature of a bike is how it fits the rider. Performance, comfort, and the risk of injury can be affected by variations of as little as 6 mm (¼ in) in your riding position, so take care to establish your bike size and riding position. Mountain bikes are made for vigorous riding; a balanced fit that distributes the rider's weight equally is essential. Try out different bikes to get a feel of what suits you best. Stick to your correct riding position, even if it feels uncomfortable at first; the body's muscles take a little time to adapt.

Position head so front hub is obscured by handlebars when looking down

Arms should be slightly bent at elbows to allow for shock absorption, with wrists kept straight

Mountain bike riding position

Back should have forward lean of at least 45°, so stronger gluteus muscles in buttocks and lower back can be used for pedalling power. Keep back straight for easy breathing

When riding, widest part of foot should be directly over pedal axle. Rider's weight should be centred between the wheels

RACING BIKE POSITION

To achieve the optimum racing bike riding position, make sure you have the correct drop handlebar extension. Too short an extension causes the back to arch, compressing the diaphragm and impairing aerobic cycling performance. Too long an extension results in locked elbows and back strain. With the saddle at the correct height, 9–13 cm (3½–5 in) of seat post should be exposed. Keep your body forwards when riding on the flat, and shift your weight back when climbing. This gives additional pedalling power.

Relaxed but straight back

Arms slightly bent

Knee remains slightly bent on downstroke

FITTING THE BIKE TO THE RIDER

For mountain biking and racing, a rider should use the smallest frame that fits. Small frames save weight and are stiffer and more responsive. For touring, a larger frame provides more stability on descents and corners. The vital factors in sizing a bike are saddle height (see p.14), the length of the top tube, the amount of seat post exposed when the saddle height is correct, and the clearance between your crotch and the top tube. These factors will vary depending on the type of bike and the rider's own physique. Standard advice on sizing a mountain bike recommends that the bike is 2–4 in smaller than the rider's road bike frame size. For safety, you need to be able to move the bike around beneath you without bashing your thighs, and to have the confidence to take a fall without serious injury, so a smaller frame makes sense.

Top tube

CROTCH-TOP TUBE CLEARANCE

The bike shown above is too big for the rider. For off-road riding, there should be at least 8–10 cm (3–4 in) clearance between the rider's crotch and the top tube, and at least 2.5 cm (1 in) clearance for commuting or touring.

Knee
slightly
bent

Adjustable
bicycle fitting
machine

CHECK SADDLE HEIGHT

Make the following quick and simple checks
to find out whether your saddle is at the right
height: first, sitting on the saddle with the ball
of your foot on the pedal and the pedal down,
your knee should be slightly bent (left);
secondly, if you can feel your hips rocking
from side to side when pedalling, your saddle
is too high, and should be adjusted.

Line

Plumb bob

FORE AND AFT POSITION OF SADDLE

Sit on the saddle with both cranks parallel to
the ground. Using a plumb bob line, move the
saddle backwards or forwards until the line
between the bony part of your knee and the
centre of the pedal axle matches the plumb
bob line. Secure the saddle in this postion.
From this point, you can set the saddle 1 cm
(⅜ in) forward for high cadence (pedalling
rate), and 1–2 cm (⅜–¾ in) back for power.

SADDLE TILT

To alter saddle tilt, you need to adjust the
angle of the seat clamp. Conventional
seat clamp bolts (right) are adjusted with
spanners, while micro-adjust seat clamp bolts
(far right) are adjusted with a 6 mm Allen key.
First use a spirit level (above) to set the saddle
in a completely level position. Now try the
saddle out. Lower the saddle nose slightly if
you feel uncomfortable. Lowering the saddle
too far will strain your arms and back. Setting
the nose too high will also hurt in time.

Seat
bolts

Micro-
adjust
bolt

Conventional seat clamp   Micro-adjust seat clamp

STEM HEIGHT

On a racing bike, the height of the stem should place the handlebars 2.5–7.6 cm (1–3 in) below the saddle, and 2.5–5 cm (1–2 in) below the saddle on a mountain bike. To adjust stem height on all bikes, loosen the stem bolt, then tap it with a hammer and wooden block to dislodge the stem. Grease the stem and replace it at the correct height. (Most stems have a mark indicating maximum safe extension.) Tighten the stem bolt firmly. The handlebars should be secure, but able to move if the bike falls.

Stem

Stem bolt

Toe clip

Toe strap

PEDALS

Always pedal with the widest part of your foot over the pedal axle for the most riding power. Make sure there is a gap of at least 5 mm ($\frac{3}{16}$ in) between the tips of your shoes and your toe clips. If you use slotted cleat or step-in clipless pedals, align the cleats with the natural rotation of your feet. Loosen the cleat mounting bolts so the cleats will move as your feet twist. Ride in various positions until you feel most comfortable. Lift slotted cleats off carefully and tighten the mounting bolts. Ask a friend to tighten the bolts on clipless pedals, as you cannot disengage your feet without disturbing the cleats.

HANDLEBARS

Mountain bike handlebar widths range from 21–24 in, and should be at least as wide as your shoulders. (The range for road bars is 38–44 cm). Wider bars give better slow-speed control (vital for off-road riding): narrower bars suit racing and sqeezing through tight gaps in traffic. Brake levers should always be positioned correctly to reduce strain on hands and forearms.

Brake lever housing

Brake lever

RACING BIKE BRAKES

Position brake lever mounts so the tips of the levers just touch a straightedge laid along the handlebar end.

MOUNTAIN BIKE BRAKES

The key to correct mountain bike brake lever position is a straight wrist. Brake using middle and index fingers only.

Tools for the Job

THE KEY TO EFFECTIVE bike maintenance and repair is good organization. Find a comfortable, well lit, and preferably warm space to work in, with a workbench or table. You will also need a means to hold the bike up, with the wheels off the ground, the right tools for your type of bike and components, parts if necessary, cleaning equipment, and lubricants required for the job. Use good-quality, purpose-specific tools. Cheap tools are frustrating to use (they may be made of inferior metals that can bend under stress) and they can damage a bike. Keep your tools in toolboxes so you know where everything is, especially your 2 mm Allen keys! It is also worth investing in an economical bike stand like those shown below; being able to turn the back wheel and cranks makes working on the transmission much easier. If you have several bikes, an advanced workstand (see p.19) is worthwhile – or share one with friends.

Adjuster

Chain stay hook

Clamp

Height adjuster

TRIPOD STAND

The *Kestrel Trio* is a simple, inexpensive stand that holds the bike by the stays, permitting transmission adjustments and removal of the rear wheel. Light and portable, it can also serve as a convenient parking stand.

WORKBENCH STAND

Most workbench manufacturers include a stand such as the *Kestrel*, which can be clamped into a vice-grip type workbench. The stand lifts the bike to a comfortable height, so that you can stand up as you work on it.

HOME WORKSHOP

The tools pictured here are the basic essentials of your home workshop. Invest in good-quality tools; you do not need many, and good tools are much easier to work with. Some of the tools are bike-specific, and should be available at most good bike shops. Those tools that are not bike-specific should be available at your local hardware or auto store. Many of the tools are reasonably lightweight and can be carried on a long ride. If you are riding in a group, carry one set for everyone to use.

Y-socket tool is a handy combined tool with 8 mm, 9 mm, and 10 mm sockets

Cable cutter will cut through cable wire and cable housing

Pin spanners are lightweight and are used for gaining access to bottom brackets

Allen (hex) keys are compulsory bike tools. Six sizes (2 mm, 2.5 mm, 3 mm, 4 mm, 5 mm, and 6 mm) should cover most of your needs

Crank extractor has to match or be made by the same manufacturer as your cranks. You cannot remove your cranks without one

Spoke key is used for replacing and tensioning spokes

Chain tool is essential for chain adjustments. If you have a unique chain, you will need a matching chain tool

Ring spanners (right and above right) are useful tools. Equip yourself with a range of sizes: 8 mm, 9 mm, 10 mm, 11 mm, 12 mm, 13 mm, 14 mm, 15 mm, 16 mm, and 17 mm

Cone spanners – the two essential sizes are 13/14 mm and 15/16 mm. Have at least two of each size

Large screwdriver is handy to use as a lever

Adjustable spanners – 4 in and 6 in sizes are useful and easy to carry around. Avoid cheap varieties

PROFESSIONAL TOOLS

The tools illustrated here are specialized, well made from strong materials, and designed for extremely effective and repeated use. Professional-quality tools are used constantly by full-time bike mechanics for every job, so have been engineered for ease and comfort of use, and complete dependability. Unfortunately, tools such as these tend to be expensive, with the exception of the freewheel remover, and worth the investment only if you ride frequently and enjoy servicing your bike regularly. Use your tools carefully, to avoid over-tightening bolts and stripping threads.

Pump handle

Flexible air tube

Air chamber

Nozzle for attaching to tyre valve

Ratchet spanner

Fixed cup and pin spanner

Headset and pedal spanner

Headset and lockring spanner

Lockring and headset spanner

Lockring spanner

Purpose-specific spanners like those above are great to use and will not bend, get damaged, or, more to the point, damage any of your bike parts

Freewheel remover (above) should fit your freewheel exactly, otherwise the remover could cause damage

Track pump – a heavy-duty pump with a bigger chamber than a hand pump; makes inflating tyres quick and effective

Deluxe crank extractor has a built-in handle for convenience

Bench vice – although not a bike-specific tool, a bench vice is very useful as a means of securing parts of a bike while you work on them. The vice should be clamped to a workbench or sturdy wooden table

Rotating clamp

Rotating clamp

Blackburn workstand

Stand

Stand

Park PCS-1 workstand

PRO-QUALITY WORKSTANDS

Freestanding adjustable workstands like those shown here are the ideal way to hold a bike in position while you work on it from all sides. The clamps attach on to any of the bike's main frame tubes. Some stands have rotating clamps, enabling you to work on the bike from almost any angle.

MULTI-TOOLS

The bike-specific combination tools shown here are lightweight and compact. They are the ideal tools to include in a basic contingency tool kit; the variety of sockets and removable heads included in them should cover most of the adjustments you may need to make while out on a ride.

Cool Tool comprises Allen keys, cone spanner, crank tool, chain breaker, headset spanner, and bottom bracket tool

Multi-socket palm tool is a multi-purpose tool with detachable Allen key and screwdriver heads, and a range of socket sizes between 8 mm and 14 mm

Six-in-one tool has Phillips and flat-blade screwdrivers, with 3 mm, 4 mm, 5 mm, and 6 mm Allen keys

Brakes

A WIDE VARIETY OF BRAKE systems are available, including drum and disc brakes, which work on wheel hubs. The most common are cable-activated caliper brakes (cantilever, side-pull, and centre-pull brakes), which work on the rim. There are also advanced hydraulic-activated caliper brakes. Before servicing your brakes, always make the following basic checks. First, ensure the rims are true (see pp.32–33) and in good condition; if they are streaked and dirty, clean them with steel wool. Check the brake blocks for wear, removing any grit. Inspect the cables and cable housing for damage. Replace any old or suspect components. After servicing brakes, test with hard braking: transfer your body weight to the pedals as soon as you brake, lifting your rear end backwards out of the saddle. Apply rear and front brakes just short of skidding or being pitched over the handlebars.

Cable housing

Cable

Straddle yoke

Straddle wire

Brake arm

Brake block

Brake pivot bolt

Brake mounting boss

Ferrule

Brake cable housing

Brake cable wire

Barrel nipple

Straddle wire

Cable grab

BRAKE CABLES

Cables must obviously be in good condition to transmit pressure from the lever to the brake arms effectively. If at all frayed or kinked they might snap under sudden load, such as an emergency stop. Make sure you buy cables with the correct diameter and type of nipple for your brake lever, typically pear nipples for road brakes and barrel nipples for cantilevers.

Barrel adjuster

Lever

Reach adjuster

Lever pivot point

Mounting clamp

BRAKE LEVERS

Mountain bike brake levers come in two- or four-finger designs, and are fitted with barrel (cable) and reach adjusters. Position brake levers pointing slightly down from the handlebars, so that a couple of fingers can rest on them constantly, while the wrist remains straight.

Brake lever

Cable housing

Cable

Straddle yoke

Cable anchor bolt

Brake block

Straddle wire

Brake arm

Brake mounting boss

Brake pivot bolt

Brake arm

Brake post mounting bolt

Brake block

Brake post

Pivot point

CANTILEVER BRAKES

Although cantilever brakes vary in design, the basic mechanics are the same. They are rigidly mounted on bosses integral to the forks or stays, which place them near the wheel rims and thus improves performance. Recent "in-board" cantilever designs feature steeply angled brake arms, so giving cleaner lines without sacrificing perfomance.

Cable Changes

SMOOTH-RUNNING, WELL LUBRICATED cables are essential for sensitive bike control. You will find that regular servicing and replacement make cable breakages a rare occurrence. For brakes, especially on mountain bikes and hybrids, use the thickest cables your system will accept. Thicker cables are stronger and less likely to stretch, and they have a positive and responsive feel. Brake and gear changing cable systems vary from bike to bike, but their maintenance is basically similar. In Britain, the left-hand lever is often used for the rear brake. In many other parts of the world, the right-hand lever is used.

ANATOMY

Straddle wire

Cable grab

Cable wire

Nipple

Cable housing

Straddle yoke

Ferrule

CABLE CUTTING

Do not cut off any excess cable wire until it has been threaded through the housing and the cable anchor bolt. (Cutting can cause the end of the wire to splay, making it difficult to thread.)

TRIMMING CABLE HOUSING

Cut the exterior vinyl sheath with a knife to expose the metal housing, then trim it to fit between the guides on the frame.

THE RIGHT TOOLS

Use good-quality wire cutters – pliers will fray the cable. Never saw through the cable; for a clean edge, snap the cutters shut sharply.

CABLE ENDS

When the cable wire has been installed and the excess trimmed, crimp a cable end-cap on to the end with pliers to stop it fraying.

FITTING A NEW CABLE – CANTILEVER BRAKES

1 ATTACH CABLE TO BRAKE LEVER

Insert the cable wire nipple into the brake lever, and nest the cable housing securely in the barrel adjuster. Run the cable through the guides fitted to the frame – these vary from bike to bike – down to the straddle yoke.

Nipple | Cable wire | Barrel adjuster

Yoke anchor bolt

Straddle yoke

2 CONNECT THE STRADDLE YOKE

Make sure the ends of the cable housing are securely fitted in their stops. Thread the wire through the small hole in the yoke anchor bolt. Holding the bolt still with a 10 mm spanner (if the bolt turns, the wire may kink), tighten the yoke anchor nut. Do this before connecting the straddle wire. The yoke height alters the angle between the straddle wire and brake arms; this angle affects braking character (see p.25).

Straddle wire

Brake arm pinch bolt

3 CONNECT THE STRADDLE WIRE

Slot the straddle wire grab end into the brake arm seat, then pass the wire through the U-shaped groove in the yoke and thread it through the pinch bolt on the opposite brake arm. Keeping the brake blocks pressed against the rim, take up the slack in the wire by pulling it through the pinch bolt. Now tighten the pinch bolt. New cables should be stretched and the brakes adjusted again (see p.25).

ALTERNATIVE STRADDLES

There are a number of small variations in straddle system design. The recent *Shimano* type shown here dispenses with the need for the cable wire to be clamped at the straddle yoke. The grab end of the small straddle wire slots into the brake arm seat. The cable wire is then threaded through the yoke and the small sleeve that extends from it. The end of the cable wire is then pulled through and tightened at the pinch bolt (taking up the slack as in Step 3, above). This system has the advantage of automatically setting the straddle at the correct angle for optimum brake performance.

Straddle yoke

Straddle wire

Sleeve

Brake Blocks

THE IMPORTANCE OF HAVING correctly positioned and well maintained brake blocks cannot be underestimated, especially if you ride a lot in wet and muddy conditions. This applies to all brakes. Faulty brakes could result in a nasty accident, so check, adjust, and service them regularly. Brake block adjustment can be rather fiddly, and inevitably there is some trial and error involved, but it is worth being as precise as you can. A wide variety of brake blocks are available, from traditional rubber blocks to hard, high-friction synthetic blocks. Remember always to replace brake blocks in pairs.

ANATOMY

Mounting post/stud

Setting lines

Braking contact area

Pair of *Aztec* brake blocks

Shimano M-system brake block

Scott/Mathauser "superbrake" block

HIGH-PERFORMANCE BRAKE SHOES
The *Shimano* and *Scott/Mathauser* brake blocks shown here are extremely effective in the wet. The *Scott/Mathauser* block has a relatively small contact area, but is made of very hard rubber, while the *Shimano* block compensates for using a softer rubber by having a large braking contact area. Some long blocks are manufactured with a curve that matches the contour of the wheel rim.

Straddle yoke

Straddle wire

Arm

Block

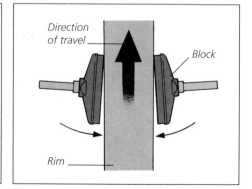

Direction of travel

Block

Rim

BRAKE BLOCK POSITION
When activated, brake blocks must press accurately against the wheel rim, as shown above. If they are too low on the rim, they could slip and foul the spokes; if too high, they may dig into the tyre.

BRAKE BLOCK TOE-IN
Slight slack in the cantilever mechanism allows brake blocks to twist a little when activated. To compensate, there should be a 1 mm (¹⁄₁₆ in) or so gap between the rim and the rear of a block when the front of the block is touching the rim.

CANTILEVER BRAKE BLOCK ADJUSTMENT

1 POSITION BLOCKS
Loosen each block locknut with a spanner to allow manual adjustment. Position each block relative to the wheel rim. Use the setting lines on the block mounting posts to set the blocks evenly. With the appropriate Allen key, hold the blocks in place while retightening the locknut. This secures them in their optimum position. Apply brake levers to test, and readjust if necessary.

2 CENTRE BRAKES
Cantilever brake tension should be distributed equally (centred) between both brake arms. *Shimano* cantilever brakes are easily centred by means of a small centring screw embedded in the right-hand side of one brake arm only. Adjust the screw using a 2 mm Allen key. Test the tension by pulling on the brake levers. Readjust the centring screw if necessary.

BRAKE SERVICING

Cantilever brake arms pivot on bosses that need to be kept clean and greased. If a boss is scarred, smooth it with emery paper and steel wool. Do this lightly; if you make the boss smaller, the brake arm will fit loosely and hamper performance. When replacing brake arms, do not tighten pivot bolts too much, as this can cause binding.

BRAKE ARM REMOVAL
Once the straddle wire is disengaged, reducing tension on the brake arms, undo the pivot mounting bolts with an Allen key to remove the arms.

SPRING TENSION
The choice of hole on the brake arm boss dictates the tension in the brake arm spring. Use more tension in muddy or wintry conditions.

Road Brakes

THE BRAKE SYSTEMS used on lightweight road-racing bikes are usually cable-activated side-pull caliper-action brakes with single or dual pivot points. Side-pull brakes combine light weight with precise performance, and work effectively on lightweight racing bikes, but are not suited to heavily-laden touring and commuting bikes, which are typically equipped with centre-pull or cantilever brakes.

Cable housing

Barrel adjuster

Quick-release tab

Brake arm

Pivot point

SIDE-PULL CABLE CHANGE

Brake lever housing

Nipple

Brake lever

1 REMOVE CABLE
Turn the barrel adjuster fully home (clockwise). Undo the cable anchor bolt with an Allen key. Remove the cable end-cap, depress the brake lever and extract the cable wire. Replace the cable housing if it is damaged or frayed (see p.44).

Cable anchor bolt

Brake block mounting bolt

2 REPLACE CABLE
Once greased, thread the new cable wire through the brake lever and cable housing, rotating it to stop the strands fraying. Seat the wire in the anchor bolt and do it up firmly. Close the quick-release tab and depress the brake lever a couple of times to stretch the cable. If there is still play, keep the caliper arm compressed against the wheel rim, then undo and reset the anchor bolt.

CALIPER ADJUSTMENT

Philips screwdriver

Adjustment screw

1 CENTRE BRAKES
Both brake blocks should strike the rim at the same time, which requires the caliper action of the brakes to be centred. For *Shimano* dual pivot bolt brakes, centre brakes by adjusting the centring adjustment screw as shown. To centre single pivot bolt brakes, undo the pivot bolt nut behind the forks, then position and hold the brake arms steady while retightening the bolt.

2 FINE-TUNE BRAKES
If there is any play or binding in the brakes (both dual pivot and single pivot types), adjust the pivot bolts. Undo locknuts with a spanner, turn the pivot bolts home (clockwise), then reverse them slightly. Hold bolts in place with an Allen key and redo locknuts. Check brake action and readjust if you need to. Periodically disassemble, clean, and grease pivot bolts.

BRAKE BLOCK SET-UP
All side-pull brake blocks have a single mounting bolt. Undo the locknuts to position the blocks. Ensure locknuts do not twist the blocks out of line when redone. If blocks do twist, undo the nuts and set blocks slightly askew. Redo nuts.

TOE-IN WITH WASHER
Toe-in cannot normally be adjusted on side-pull brakes. You can, however, use a dished or shaped washer in the brake block mounting bolt set-up. Set the washer in a position where it alters the angle at which the block will strike the wheel rim.

Locknut

Washer

Dished washer

Brake block

Brake arm

TRADITIONAL TOE-IN METHOD
This effective traditional method involves manually bending the brake arms with an adjustable spanner in one smooth movement. Ensure that the jaws of the spanner grip the brake arm firmly. There is a risk of metal fatigue, so practise the technique with caution.

Wheels and Tyres

A BICYCLE WHEEL IS A SOPHISTICATED engineering design, and despite its light weight and the relative weakness of its individual parts, it is an incredibly strong structure. The tension of the spokes, which are usually made of stainless steel, pulls, or compresses, the wheel rim inwards towards the centre of the wheel, and this is the secret of the wheel's strength. Different arrangements of spoke patterns, for example, two-, three-, and four-cross tangential patterns, are used to increase the strength of the wheel's resistance to pedalling and braking forces. The rims are also designed to provide the primary surface for braking, and are hollow in cross-section (similar to box girders), which enhances strength but is also lightweight. Never underestimate the importance of keeping wheels true and well maintained – a faulty wheel can be potentially lethal. So check wheels and tyres thoroughly before every ride.

Rim

Nipple

Tyre wall

Spoke

Tread

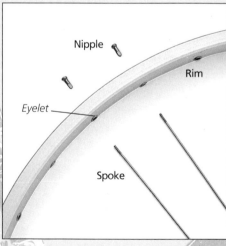

Nipple

Rim

Eyelet

Spoke

RIMS AND SPOKES

Good bike rims have eyelets that prevent the spoke nipples jumping through the rim. Spokes should always be evenly tensioned on each side of the wheel for the wheel to be true (see pp.32–33). Measure an old spoke accurately, or take one with you when you are buying new ones at a bike shop, as they come in hundreds of different lengths. Your tool kit should always include a spoke key.

Bead

Tread

Tyre

Valve
lockring

Valve

Valve
dust-cap

Inner tube

TYRES AND TUBES

There is now a bewildering array of bike tyres on the market, especially for mountain bikes. For optimum performance and durability, ensure that the width of the tyres you buy matches the width of your rims. When you replace tubes, take an old one to the bike shop with you, and make sure you buy tubes with the correct type of valve fitted. To save having to mend a puncture when you are out on a ride, always carry a spare inner tube with you.

Braking surface

Tread

Tyre wall

Rim

Nipple

Spoke

Spokes and Trueing

BIKE WHEELS USUALLY have 32 or 36 spokes, and are built using radial or, most commonly, tangential spoke arrangements. The spokes in a radial pattern, which is rare on production bikes, literally radiate from the hub to the rim, making the wheel light with minimal wind resistance (drag). In a tangential pattern the spokes cross over each other obliquely (as in the photos below), so that torque is better transmitted from acceleration or braking. Spokes are made from steel: chrome- or nickel-plated, galvanized rustless, or stainless.

ANATOMY

Spoke nipple

Thread

Plain gauge spoke

SPOKE THICKNESS

Spokes are available in butted and non-butted (plain gauge) form. Butted spokes are thicker at the ends than in the middle, making the wheel lighter and more resilient.

REPLACING A DAMAGED OR BROKEN SPOKE

Flange

New spoke

Rim

1 INSERT NEW SPOKE

First take the tyre and tube off the wheel. Remove rim tape from inside the rim if there is any. If the spoke is damaged but still intact, unscrew the nipple and pull the spoke out at the hub flange. If the spoke is broken, remove any fragments at each end. Push the end of the new spoke through the empty eye in the flange – this may mean coming through the wheel from the other side, as the spokes run alternately to the inside and the outside of the flange – until the elbow and spoke head catch.

2 THREAD NEW SPOKE

Examine how the spokes are laced in relation to each other, according to the tangential spoke arrangement. With the spoke head flush with the flange, weave the spoke into place, mimicking the arrangement of the spoke next door but one (alternate spokes follow the same lacing pattern). Do not force the spoke – it should flex quite easily if you apply gentle pressure.

Elbow

Spoke head

Nipple

Screwdriver

3 TENSION SPOKE

Thread the end of the spoke through the eyelet in the rim, then push the nipple on to the end. Oil the nipple with a light penetrating lubricant to prevent the nipple and the spoke thread binding. Screw the nipple on to the spoke with a screwdriver. Tighten the spoke to approximately the same tension as the other spokes on the wheel. File down any spoke ends protruding into the rim.

4 TRUE THE WHEEL

Unless the wheel is virtually brand new, replacing a damaged or broken spoke will inevitably put the wheel out of true. Follow the procedures for assessing how much a wheel is out of true and then for trueing it, as described on pp.32–33.

SPOKELESS WHEELS

Wheels are made with spokes to save weight. However, as the wheels spin, the spokes churn the air, generating aerodynamic drag. To overcome drag, designers have created wheels like the disc wheel and the tri-spoke wheel, which smooth the flow of air. Although heavier than spoked wheels, these wheels are much faster and require less energy at high speeds. Disc wheels are only used at the rear, where they are effectively shielded by the rider's legs and the frame tubes – at the front, they would act like a sail, making the bike very difficult to handle. The spokes on tri-spoke wheels act like airfoils, and tri-spokes are used at both the front and rear.

Disc wheel

Tri-spoke wheel

CHECKING THE WHEELS

CHECKING WHEELS FOR TRUEING

Wheel trueing is an art more than a science, so as a beginner you should not expect perfection at your first attempt. Each spoke should be checked for bends and breaks. Check for even tension by plucking the mid-point of each of the spokes and listening to the note produced. Front wheel spokes should all sound the same if the tension is even all round. On the rear wheel, the spokes on the freewheel side of the hub have more tension than the spokes opposite. If any are too tight, loosen them until they feel and sound the same as the others on the same side.

TRACKING

An important step when examining your bike wheels is to check the tracking. This simply means checking the alignment of the wheels relative to each other, along a centre line dictated by the top tube. Turn the bike upside down so it rests on its saddle and handlebars. Make sure the handlebars are set straight ahead. Sit behind one of the wheels so that, at eye level, you can see whether the wheels are in line. (See also p.86.)

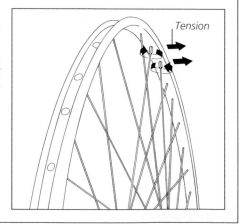

Top tube

BALANCING TENSION AT THE RIM

Obtaining even tension on front wheel rims is easier than rear wheel rims, because the spokes on both sides of the front wheel hub are at the same angle, and tensioned equally in order to keep the rim central. Back wheel rims also run centrally, but over the length of the hub and freewheel. The flange on the freewheel side of the wheel is not at the edge of the hub, so there are different spoke angles on either side of the wheel, giving a dish shape. To ensure equal rim tension, work a ½ turn at a time, balancing each side. If you loosen one spoke by a ½ turn, tighten its opposite by the same amount.

Tension

TRUEING A WHEEL

Chalk

1 MARK UP THE WHEEL

Mark lateral high spots (points where the rim is most out of true) by holding chalk or a marker against one of the stays while the wheel is spinning. Slowly bring the chalk in until it comes into contact with the high points on the rim. The longest mark made by the chalk indicates the area where the spokes need adjusting first.

2 LATERALLY ADJUST

Even tension is vital, so adjust any spoke in the marked area that is out of step with the others. Loosen the spokes that lead to the hub flange on the same side as the mark; tighten those leading to the opposite flange. Spin the wheel to check progress. With the first mark corrected, move to the next longest mark.

Spoke key

WHEEL STANDS

If possible, use a wheel stand to check and true wheels. Faults can be better measured and adjusted than rough-trueing using the dropouts. Wheel stands have adjustable reference pointers that help you judge lateral and vertical truth.

Base

Lateral truth pointer

Vertical truth pointer

Chalk mark indicates lateral high spot

3 VERTICALLY ADJUST

Mark vertical high spots by holding a marker over the top of the rim and spinning the wheel. Where there are high spots, tighten the spokes in groups of four; with flat spots, loosen the spokes. Work slowly, tightening spokes only a little at a time for accuracy.

4 FINE-TUNE ADJUSTMENTS

After making any vertical adjustments, check again for side-to-side play, and correct by adjusting the spokes again if necessary. Remove any rim tape from the inside of the rim and look for any protruding spokes that might puncture the inner tube. File these down before replacing the rim tape.

Tyres and Tubes

DEPENDING ON WHAT TYPE of cycling you enjoy most, it is worth experimenting with different types of tyres. Mountain bike tyres are usually measured in inches, and road tyres either in inches or metrically. The most common mountain bike tyre size is 26 in diameter, with tread widths varying from 1–2.7 in. When you choose a tyre at a bike shop, pick one that is easy to take off your bike rim. Also keep a stock of right-size inner tubes at hand.

ANATOMY

Knobbly lug

Tyre wall | Tyre bead

Treadless slick tyre

Multi-purpose *Nimbus* tyre

Knobbly rear tyre

DIFFERENT TREAD PATTERNS

The three types of mountain bike tyre tread pattern shown here are the most commonly available ones for different conditions of use. The treadless slick provides optimal grip on asphalt and concrete, giving a comfortable ride with minimal rolling resistance and low tyre noise. The multi-purpose *Nimbus* tyre is a lightweight all-round performance tyre that is very stable in wet weather. It is suitable for hard-packed off-road surfaces, but not mud. The knobbly rear tyre is designed to cope with all off-road situations. The widely spaced lugs discharge mud and small stones easily, while the horizontal central bands provide much-needed traction during acceleration.

Presta valve | Schraeder valve

VALVES

Loosen the barrel on a Presta valve to inflate the tube. A car pump can be used to inflate a tube with a Schraeder valve.

TUBES

In addition to the conventional butyl rubber tube shown here, other types of tube are available. So-called "puncture proof" tubes are filled with a synthetic liquid sealant, and although this tends to make them heavy and harsh to ride, they can be useful for commuting. Latex tubes are very light and are widely used in racing. Despite their light weight, their elasticity makes them surprisingly puncture-resistant.

Inner tube

Valve

Valve locknut/ring

Dust-cap

Two-minute Tube Change

1 Remove the Valve

Undo the valve dust-cap and locknut. On the Presta valve, undo the valve and push it in to completely deflate the tube. On a Schraeder valve, use a pen, screwdriver, or other small implement to push in the valve. Press the valve stem through the hole in the rim.

Valve

Tyre bead

Rim well

2 Free the Tyre

Pinch the tyre walls firmly together all the way round the tyre, pushing them back and forth to work the tyre bead away from the rim. The tyre and rim should then separate easily. Make sure the beads on each side are down in the rim well. If necessary, raise the tube valve clear of the bead.

3 Unhook the Tyre

If the tyre is a loose fit, it should be possible to lift one side over the rim with your hands. If the tyre is tight, carefully insert a tyre lever, making sure not to pinch the tube, and lever the tyre bead over the rim. Work all around the rim until one wall of the tyre is completely off the rim.

Tyre lever

4 Remove the Inner Tube

Lift the valve out through the valve hole, being careful not to damage the threads on the valve body. Remove the tube from the tyre. If you need to repair a puncture, follow the instructions on p.37. If you are replacing the tube with a new one, check it is clean, dry, and the correct size.

5 Check the Tyre

Feel along the inside and outside of the tyre with your fingers. Remove any embedded foreign bodies before inserting a new or repaired tube. If the tube is punctured on the rim side, the cause may be a protruding spoke. If you cannot file the spoke down, cover it with several layers of tape. Turn the page for Step 6.

TUBE CHANGE continued

6 REPLACE THE TUBE
Partially inflate the replacement or repaired tube. This makes the tube easier to work with, as it has enough shape to avoid being creased, wrinkled, or pinched when you replace the tyre. Place the tube inside the tyre and insert the valve stem through the valve hole in the rim, making sure it is straight. Then thread the valve locknut or ring loosely on to the stem.

Tube
Valve stem

Tyre bead

7 REPLACE THE TYRE
Tuck the rest of the tube carefully into the tyre, ensuring it is evenly spread all the way around the inside of the tyre, then deflate it completely. Push the valve stem up into the tyre as far as the locknut. Slip the tyre bead over the rim. Keep the valve stem clear of the rim or the bead may catch on it, creating a bulge in the tyre that may damage the tube.

8 SECURE THE TYRE
Press the side of the tyre over the rim with your thumbs. Work back and forth rhythmically to prevent the tyre popping off at either side. Knead the tyre with a steady pressure; if you feel it getting very tight, reach across it and yank it firmly into place. Check the tube has not been pinched between the rim and the tyre, then reinflate it fully.

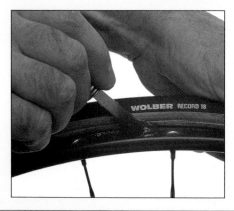

WOLBER RECORD 18

TUBULAR TYRES
To save weight and maintain high pressure, professional racing cyclists often use tubular tyres ("tubs"), which are tube and tyre in one. The tyre casings are sewn together with the tube inside, and the tyre is then glued to the rim. The casings are made of cotton or silk, and the tread vulcanized (heat-treated) either by machine or hand. Riders then have to let the tyres dry out to the right consistency: too moist and they may pick up grit, and puncture; too dry and the tyre may slip. However, advances in conventional tyre design has made tubs a rarity on racing bikes.

REPAIRING A PUNCTURE

You need a repair kit with patches and a tube of glue; sandpaper and chalk are also recommended. The key to a successful repair is thorough preparation and cleanliness. If your hands get dirty when you remove the wheel, clean them so that no oil gets on the inner tube. To locate the puncture, inflate the tube and hold it next to your face, and rotate it. If you cannot feel or hear any air escaping, test the valve with a drop of spit. If you still cannot trace the hole, fully inflate the tube, immerse it in water, and watch for air bubbles.

Rubber cement

Rectangular repair patch

Round repair patches

1 PREPARE THE TUBE
Once you have found the puncture, dry the tube and roughen the area around the puncture with sandpaper. This helps the rubber cement adhere to the surface. Make the sanded area larger than the repair patch. If you do not have any sandpaper, a coarse, flat stone surface will do, such as concrete. Give the tube one last thorough clean.

2 APPLY THE CEMENT
Clean your hands. Spread an even layer of rubber cement over the sanded area. Let the cement dry until tacky, so that the solvent in the cement evaporates. Do not allow anything to touch the cement during this time. With the tube in a safe place, check the tyre for damage while you wait (see Step 5, p.35).

3 PATCH THE PUNCTURE
Peel off the foil on the patch, being careful not to touch the adhesive area that you expose. Press the patch firmly and centrally down over the puncture hole, rubbing from the centre to the edges. Use sandpaper to powder the chalk, sprinkling it over any excess cement around the patch.

4 FINAL CHECK
Leave the patch to set for a couple of minutes, then pinch the tube and patch together so that the cellophane back of the patch splits. Peel the cellophane away from the centre without peeling off the patch. Inflate the tube, and check the patch. Replace the tube and the tyre (see p.36).

Transmission

THE TERM TRANSMISSION IS USED to describe those mechanical parts of a bike that work in unison to transmit the cyclist's pedalling power to the bike's wheels by means of a system of gears. Transmission systems typically include a shift lever, cables, and the gear changing mechanism, of which there are two kinds: internal rear hub changer (most famous being the long-lived, three-speed *Sturmey Archer* model used on utility bikes), and those featuring front and rear derailleurs, standard issue on mountain and road bikes. Almost all bikes today are equipped with a gear changing mechanism, except track-racing bikes and some time-trial bikes, which have a single chainring and one fixed (non-freewheeling) cog on the rear wheel; the cranks do not stop rotating when the rider stops pedalling, so the rider has to keep moving with the pedals until the bike comes to a halt.

Guide pulley

Derailleur body

Barrel adjuster

Cable anchor bolt

Derailleur cage

Tension pulley

Rear gear cable housing

Freewheel sprockets/cogs

Rear derailleur

REAR DERAILLEUR

As the chain comes off the bottom of a front chainring it passes through the rear derailleur on jockey wheels (the tension pulley and guide pulley). The cage holding the wheels is fixed to the main body of the changer by a pivot, and is held under constant spring tension to keep the chain taut. The side-to-side travel of the derailleur cage is limited by adjustable screws.

FREEWHEEL

Freewheels divide into two categories: those that are part of the wheel hub, and others that are cassettes that slide or thread on to the hub. The freewheel has a central body on to which the sprockets are threaded, or slide on splines.

Gear cable anchor bolt

Mounting clamp

Outer cage plate

Inner cage plate

Cage screw

Barrel adjuster

Thumb-shifter lever

Gear indicator

Friction/indexed shifting switch

Mounting clamp

FRONT DERAILLEUR

This consists of a metal cage through which the chain passes as it feeds on to the front chainrings. The cage moves from side to side, and by pressing on the side of the chain, shifts it between the chainrings. The derailleur uses a pivot system to keep the sides of the cage vertical.

THUMB-SHIFTER

Shift levers can be mounted on the down tube, the top tube, the stem, or on the handlebars. (Thumb-shifters are for handlebars only.) Cables lead from the shifters to the derailleurs, and when activated, the derailleurs move laterally, guiding the chain between freewheel sprockets or chainrings. Some modern shifters have double levers for pushing with the thumb and pulling with the forefinger.

Front derailleur

Crank bolt

Crank arm

Spider

Chainring bolt

Middle chainring

Outer chainring

Inner chainring

Chain

CHAIN

The chain should be the correct width to operate smoothly over the sprockets and chainrings, and the correct length for optimum shifting performance. Grit builds up on chains fast, so they need regular cleaning.

CRANKS AND CHAINRINGS

In contrast to the freewheel sprockets, the larger the chainring the higher the gear. Most bikes today have a series of chainrings to give a wide range of gear ratios. Cranks range in length from 165–180 mm, with 170 mm average for mountain bikes, and 175 mm average for road bikes.

Chains

CLEAN, WELL LUBRICATED CHAINS can be up to 98 per cent efficient (see p.71–72). Dirt causes link rivets to enlarge the holes in the link plates; the chain stretches and ceases to mesh smoothly with the teeth on the chainrings and sprockets. Derailleur shifting suffers, and under pressure the chain will jump. When replacing a chain, renew the chainrings and sprockets: a new chain will kick on worn sprockets. Ensure the new chain is the correct type for your transmission. Seek advice, because the quality of components can vary.

ANATOMY

Chain

Bushing

Inner link plate

Rivet head

Outer link plate

Sedis 2.38 mm standard chain

Sedis 2.38 mm gold chain

Shimano HyperGlide chain

CHAIN TYPES

Various chains have been developed for different bicycle types and uses. Five- or six-speed bicycles will have a wider chain than a seven- or eight-speed. Older, non-derailleur chains are broken at a master link, whereas the more modern type can be broken at any point along their length, using a chain tool.

BROKEN CHAINS

Exerting too much pressure on an older chain can cause one of the links to break. To repair it you must have a chain tool or rivet extractor, so always keep one in your basic tool kit (see pp.16–17). Chains, especially those on mountain bikes, take a lot of punishment. If the chain needs frequent repair, replace it.

MEASURE FOR WEAR

Test the chain for wear by lifting it up when it is on the large chainring. If one of the chainwheel teeth is fully exposed beneath it, the chain is worn out. Replace the chain, the chainrings, and the sprockets at the same time if they are worn and you can afford to; a new chain will perform badly on worn sprockets.

DISMANTLING AND REASSEMBLY

Driving pin

Spreader slot

Locating lugs

Handle

Arm

Standard chain tool or rivet extractor

USING A CHAIN TOOL

Breaking and joining a chain is easy once you have the knack: begin by practising on an old length of chain. Chain rivets are very difficult to replace if they fall out completely, so take care when using the extractor not to screw rivets in too far.

1 POSITION THE CHAIN

Nest the chain in the chain tool by laying the chain flat, and slotting it firmly between the locating lugs. Then make sure the outer link plate is braced against the back of the tool. Do this by centring the driving pin exactly against the chain rivet, ensuring the chain stays in place, then slowly tighten the handle.

2 DISPLACE THE RIVET

To displace the rivet, rotate the chain tool handle 6 to 6½ turns until the rivet is clear of the inner link plate but is still just held in place by the outer link plate. Standard extractor tools like the one shown here have an open back. More expensive models have an adjustable screw that prevents the rivets being driven out too far. They may also have a longer handle arm for increased leverage. Turn the page for Step 3.

Rivet

Inner link plate

DISMANTLING AND REASSEMBLY continued

3 SEPARATE THE LINKS

Flex the chain to separate the link from its neighbour. If the rivet has not been driven out far enough, you may have to use the chain tool again to drive the rivet a little further out. Work with care, turning the handle slowly. Only rotate by ⅓ turn at a time, so that the rivet does not pop out of the outer link plate.

Bushing

Rivet

Driving pin

Rivet

4 REPLACE THE RIVET

To rejoin the links, position the chain in the tool (see Step 1, p.41), with the protruding rivet against the driving pin. Firmly tighten the handle to drive the rivet in, but if it sticks, back the driving pin off, wiggle the link to line up the rivet with the holes, and try again. Using excessive force may distort the chain or the rivet, which will result in chain malfunction.

5 POSITION THE RIVET

Stop driving the rivet in when it is just proud of the outer link plate. The rivet should also be proud of the link plate nearest the driving pin, since the process will have compressed the components together.

Outer link plate

Lug

Chain

Driving pin

6 FLEX THE LINK

Nest the chain firmly in the spreader slot (the space between the pair of lugs nearest to the tool handle), with the driving pin against the most prominent end of the rivet. Gently – ⅓ turn or so should be sufficient – tighten the handle, to move the rivet slightly further and open up the link. This process ensures that there is just enough required flexibility between the inner plate, the outer plate, and the bushing.

Jockey wheel

7 CORRECT THE CHAIN LENGTH

A new chain will not necessarily be the correct length for your transmission. Set the length of a new chain so that when it is on the largest chainring and smallest sprocket, the rear-derailleur jockey wheels align vertically. Check that the chain remains taut when the chain is on the smallest chainring and sprocket.

NON-DERAILLEUR ⅛-INCH CHAIN

This type of chain is joined by a master link. It is dismantled simply by removing the spring clip and the end-plate, then pulling the link out. When replaced, the spring clip's closed end should face the direction of travel

End-plate

Spring clip   Master link

HyperGlide chain tool

HyperGlide chain

SPECIAL CHAINS AND TOOLS

Bicycles equipped with *Shimano* groupsets are usually fitted with a HyperGlide chain. Rivets are replaceable, but a special chain tool is required.

CONNECTING RIVET

HyperGlide chains should not be broken twice in the same place. Drive the pointed end of the new rivet in with the tool, then break off the excess with pliers.

HyperGlide chain rivet

Cables

TRANSMISSION CABLES COME IN different lengths and thicknesses, and with different types of nipples. Always use the right size and type of cable, particularly for gear changing systems. Either order for your make and model of bike, or take the bike or old cables to a shop. Keep a spare set in case one breaks. Transmission cables must be good quality, especially for indexed gearing systems, since the movement at the lever must be precisely reproduced at the derailleur. If the cable wire or housing flexes or compresses, accurate gear changing is impossible.

ANATOMY

Cable wire

Barrel nipple

Cable housing

Ferrule

CABLE GUIDES

Slotted cable guides (left) are fitted to some frames. These allow the cable wires to be regreased by sliding sections of housing along the wire, thereby dispensing with the need to remove the cable completely and disturb the gear indexing.

Gently curving cable

CABLE HOUSING

Replace damaged cable housing and frayed cables as soon as possible. Cut housing to a length that gives a gentle curve between guides, notably between the handlebars and frame: this allows the wire inside to operate smoothly. If, after cutting cable housing, the ends are burred or uneven, neaten them with a file.

REPLACING TRANSMISSION CABLES

1 UNTHREAD CABLE

Undo the derailleur cable anchor bolt. Dismantle the shifter by removing the shift lever from its mounting plate or clamp. Pull out the old cable wire. Grease and thread the new wire. Reassemble the shifter. (Some shifters are so designed that they do not need dismantling; simply remove the barrel adjuster, then thread the new cable through the unit.) Ensure cable housing is snug in barrel adjusters and guides.

2 ATTACH CABLE

With the chain on the smallest chainring and sprocket, pass the cable through the derailleur anchor bolt. Tug the cable firmly and do the bolt up. Now pull on an exposed length of wire to stretch it. Take up any slack by redoing the anchor bolt. Adjust the gears (see pp.46–51). (N.B. If you are replacing the rear derailleur cable, remember to reverse the barrel adjuster on the derailleur two turns to allow for fine-tuning later.)

RECENT SHIFTER DESIGNS

Shimano's Rapid Fire and its successor, Rapid Fire Plus, are the latest in shifter design. Rapid Fire uses the thumb to operate both up- and down-shift levers. Rapid Fire Plus shifts the chain down a gear by pushing a thumb lever forward, and up a gear by pulling a separate lever back with the forefinger.

Up-shift lever

Down-shift lever

Brake lever

Rapid Fire Plus shifter

RAPID FIRE CABLE RENEWAL

Changing the cable wire is a relatively simple operation on Rapid Fire systems. Once disconnected at the derailleur, the cable wire can be pulled out of the access hole in the shifter body. Replacement is simply a case of threading the wire back down the hole. On Rapid Fire shifters the outer casing has to be removed first.

Rear Derailleur

WHEN SHIFTING GEARS, the rear derailleur moves the chain to a selected cog, aligning the chain so it runs smoothly. Early derailleurs were controlled using simple, friction-tensioned levers that the rider had to position manually. Many systems still include the option of friction shifting, but indexed and push-button shifting are now the norm. Modern derailleurs are easy to use, but they must be accurately adjusted. Side-to-side movement (travel) must be limited to stop the chain jumping off the inner and outermost cogs.

ANATOMY

Guide pulley
Body
Tension screw
Top travel-adjusting screw
Lower travel-adjusting screw
Cage
Barrel adjuster
Tension pulley

REAR DERAILLEUR TRAVEL ADJUSTMENT

Gear lever

Gear lever

1 LIMIT TRAVEL IN TOP GEAR

With the bike on a workstand or similar, pull the rear gear lever to shift the chain on to the smallest cog and the outer chainring (top gear). Slacken the top travel-adjusting screw until no resistance is felt. Screw it back in clockwise until both the jockey wheels on the derailleur align with the small sprocket when viewed from directly behind the bicycle.

2 LIMIT TRAVEL IN BOTTOM GEAR

Push the rear gear lever with your thumb to shift the chain on to the largest sprocket and smallest chainring (bottom gear). Slacken the lower travel-adjusting screw until no resistance is felt. Now the jockey wheels will probably be slightly too close to the wheel spokes. Retighten the adjusting screw until the jockey wheels and the sprocket align.

Tension
screw

3 ADJUST TENSION SCREW

Run the chain on to the largest chainring and the smallest sprocket. Rotate the cranks, and adjust the tension screw so that the guide pulley is as close to the smallest sprocket as possible, but not actually touching it. Turning the cranks again, run the chain to the smallest chainring and the largest sprocket, checking that the guide pulley does not touch any of the sprockets. Adjust again if necessary.

REAR DERAILLEUR MOUNTING

For modern rear derailleurs to work well, the rear dropouts must be aligned with each other, and the derailleur hanger must be parallel with the centre line of the bike. Frame alignment requires specific equipment and a high degree of skill, so should be done by a bike shop. As a rough test, stand behind the bike and visually check that a line through the guide and tension pulleys is parallel with (in the same plane as) the rear wheel. Derailleurs are often damaged in a crash or if the bike is dropped (see p.87).

REAR DERAILLEUR SERVICING

Undo the mounting bolt, after removing the cable at the anchor bolt, and if the chain is on the bike, remove the tension and guide pulleys. To dismantle the cage, which it rarely needs, undo the cage stop screw (which prevents the cage from unwinding) and unwind it. Make a careful note of how many times it rotates, and, when you separate the cage and arm, the position of the spring. The spring tension on most derailleurs can be adjusted by placing the end of the spring in one of a series of holes inside the derailleur body. Lubricate the pivot pins on the body, then clean and lubricate the guide and tension pulleys with a light, fast grease (see pp.72–73).

Tension pulley
pivot bolt

REAR DERAILLEUR REMOVAL

To remove the mechanism without breaking the chain, remove the tension pulley by undoing its mounting bolt with an Allen key. The guide pulley may also need loosening.

INDEXED GEAR SHIFTING ADJUSTMENT

Rear shifter

Rear gear cable

1 PREPARE THE BIKE
Mount the bike on a workstand or other device to raise the rear wheel off the ground. With the chain on the middle chainring, use the rear shifter to shift the chain on to the smallest sprocket. Slacken the rear gear cable by turning the barrel adjuster on the rear derailleur clockwise all the way home. Repeat with the barrel adjuster on the rear shifter, but this time finish off by reversing two turns to allow for fine-tuning later.

Barrel adjuster

Rear shifter

2 TENSION THE CABLE
Make one downwards shift with the rear shifter, then start to turn the cranks by hand. (Initially there will be no movement from the rear derailleur.) Begin to tension the rear gear cable by turning the barrel adjuster on the rear derailleur anti-clockwise. The intention here is to make the index positions of the shifter exactly match the sprockets, ensuring accurate and positive gear shifting. A well adjusted indexed system should make gear changes virtually silent.

Barrel
adjuster

Derailleur
cage

3 FINAL CHECK

Continue reversing the barrel adjuster while turning the cranks, until the chain finally shifts up on to the second cog (thereby matching the position of the shifter). Continue turning the adjuster until the chain begins to catch on the third sprocket, then reverse it – but only enough to stop this catching. Finally, check the shifting operation between all cogs. Fine-tune the barrel adjuster if necessary, to provide positive shifting throughout the gears.

Cage aligns with cog

THUMB-SHIFTERS

The oldest thumb-shifter gearing systems offered no indexed shifting, whereas the most modern systems are indexed only. Combined systems are a happy medium.

OLD VERSUS NEW

This older twin-function thumb-shifter design allows the rider to switch between indexed and friction shifting. This is useful if the indexing becomes faulty and for fine-tuning the derailleur's position whilst riding. More recent all-indexed designs offer slicker shifting and greater comfort, but cannot match the reliability of their predecessors.

Switch for changing
from indexed to
friction shifting

Thumb-
shifter lever

Gear cable
barrel adjuster

Front Derailleur

THE FRONT DERAILLEUR SHIFTS the chain between
the chainrings. Adjustments should be made to
it when shifting between chainrings becomes
inaccurate or noisy, and whenever the rear
derailleur is adjusted; both derailleurs have to
work together for the transmission to be effective.
So, if you adjust the front derailleur while the
chain is on the smallest chainring, the chain
should be in line at the rear (that is, on the
largest sprocket), and when on the outer
chainring, on the smallest sprocket. Adjusting
the derailleur is also an operational matter, that
is, after basic adjustments have been made with
the bike on a workstand, further fine-tuning
will be required while you are actually riding.

ANATOMY

Mounting
clamp

Travel-
adjusting
screws

Cable
anchor bolt

Inner cage
plate

Outer cage
plate

Cage
screw

Mounting
clamp bolt

Cage plate

Chainring

POSITIONING THE FRONT DERAILLEUR

The inner and outer derailleur
cage plates must be parallel
with the chainrings when
viewed from above. Undo
the mounting clamp bolt,
then carefully position the
mechanism. Tighten the
clamp, and again check the
plates against the chainrings.
If they are parallel, finally
tighten the clamp firmly, to
avoid slipping, since the
mechanism is under constant
pressure from the shifter cable.

CHECKING FOR CLEARANCE

With the cage over the large chainring, use the
mounting bolt to position the outer plate of
the cage 1–3 mm (¹⁄₁₆–¹⁄₈ in) above the chainring.
A tighter clearance is needed for the closely
spaced double chainrings, and a wider clearance
for the broadly spaced triple chainrings. If
your bike is fitted with off-round *Biopace* rings,
make adjustments with the crank pointed down
in line with the seat tube, so that the highest
part of the chainring is next to the cage plates.

FRONT DERAILLEUR TRAVEL ADJUSTMENT

1 LIMIT LEFT-HAND TRAVEL

Run the chain on to the small chainring and large sprocket. With triple chainrings, use the lower travel-adjust screw to set a clearance of 1–2 mm (¹⁄₂₄–¹⁄₁₆ in) between the inner cage plate and chain. With double chainrings, position the inner cage plate as close as possible to the chain without touching it. Test cable for slack. Tighten cable anchor bolt if needed.

2 LIMIT RIGHT-HAND TRAVEL

Run the chain to the large chainring and small sprocket. With the top travel-adjust screw, set the outer cage plate very close to but not touching the chain. On *Shimano* STI systems, run the chain to the middle chainring and large cog. Use the cable adjuster on the shift lever to position the inner cage plate close to the chain.

DERAILLEUR/CRANK CLEARANCE

After correctly adjusting the front derailleur, the crank may just clip the outer cage plate when the chain is on the large chainring. If so, gently bend the outer plate inwards with pliers, but not too far; the cage and chainring still have to align.

FRONT DERAILLEUR OPTIONS

Apart from standard bottom-pull mechanisms operated by wires threaded underneath the bottom bracket, other front derailleur system options include:

• Top-pull derailleur: in this design, the derailleur arm is pulled up from above, with the cable routed along the top tube and down the seat tube (as featured in the steps above). The benefit of this system is that the cable does not get clogged with mud, the major disadvantage of cables threaded underneath the bottom bracket.

• Bottom-pull derailleur adapted to top-pull set-up: this is done by threading the cable wire through a cable guide fixed to the derailleur arm, and allowing the cable housing to butt up against the guide. The wire is then anchored by a bolt fixed to the seat tube above the bottom bracket (as shown above). This causes the standard cable operation to be reversed, so that when the shifter is activated, the cable housing actually slides over the wire (which remains static), forcing the derailleur arm to move.

Chainset

THE CHAINSET COMPRISES the chainrings and the cranks. Periodically check the chainring teeth for damage by removing the chain, placing a light behind the chainring, and rotating it. Chipped teeth will be visible from the side, bent teeth from above. Also check the chainrings are true. They can be bent into shape with a large spanner, but it is best to get this done at a bike shop. Regularly ensure the crank bolts are snug (see below). Check the tightness of new cranks every 40 km (25 miles) for the first 320 km (200 miles) of use. See pp.62–63 for crank removal.

Chainring

Spacer

Chainring bolt

TIGHTENING CRANKS

Remove dust-caps and tighten the crank bolts with a spanner or crank tool. Tighten them firmly, but not too hard, in case the threads strip. If the bolts are alloy, first use a steel bolt to tighten the cranks, then replace the alloy bolts.

Crank mounting
bolt socket

Crank

SHIMANO
DEORE

Spider arm

Crank arm

Threaded socket
for pedal

CHECKING CRANKS

Creaking noises when riding are often caused by loose cranks. To test the cranks, position them horizontally, then press down hard on both pedals at once with your hands. Rotate the cranks 180°, then press down on the pedals again. If either crank moves, the crank mounting bolts need to be tightened.

TIGHTENING CHAINRINGS

1 CHECK THE CHAINRING BOLTS

Regularly check the tightness of the chainring bolts. Use the correct size of Allen key – usually 5 mm on most two- and three-ringed units. If the bolts are slack, tighten them.

2 TIGHTEN THE BOLTS

Move around the outer ring, tightening each bolt with equal pressure. Do not overtighten them, just take up any slack. Once they have been tightened a few times and have bedded in, secure them with a thread adhesive.

Chainring bolt

MOUNTAIN BIKE CHAINRINGS

The introduction of the mountain bike, and its use on a variety of steep terrain, has necessitated the introduction of widely spaced gear ratios. This has affected chainwheel design and led to some problems with gear changing.

Special chain guides assist smooth gear changing

GEAR CHANGING PROBLEMS

Mountain bikes use chainring sets (above) with large differences in diameter, allowing a wide range of gear ratios. This set-up requires long chains and derailleur cages, which in turn can make gear changing in either direction slower and not as smooth as on a standard set-up.

Crank arm

MODIFIED DESIGN

Some manufacturers have developed new ways to improve gear changing. *Shimano's* HyperDrive chainrings (left) have a series of shorter (drop) teeth on the two outer rings to allow the chain to drop smoothly, and extra guide teeth on their sides to help pull the chain up.

Drop tooth

Freewheel and Sprockets

A FREEWHEEL IS FORMED of two main parts, one inside the other. The inner part threads or slides on to the hub. The outer body holds the various gear cogs, or sprockets. The inside of a freewheel is an intricate maze of small ratchet pawls, ball bearings, springs, and pins. It is important to keep it clean and lubricated (see pp.71–72), so that the pawls do not become clogged and stuck. Keep one ear tuned to your freewheel; if the steady whirring sound becomes at all ragged or uneven, then you will need to service or replace the freewheel as soon as possible.

ANATOMY

Lockring

Sprocket cluster

Spline

21-tooth (T) cog

17-T   16-T   15-T   13-T

Lockring

Cassette freewheel

Spacer   19-T

14-T   12-T

Damaged tooth

Broken teeth

THREADS AND SPLINES

Freewheels divide into two main types. The threaded variety screws on to the hub complete with the cogs. The cassette freewheel is fixed to the hub with the cogs sliding on to splines (slots) on its back; a lockring secures them in place.

BROKEN SPROCKET TEETH

Sprockets come under a great deal of force from the chain when the cyclist is pedalling up steep inclines. Sprocket teeth may eventually break as a result of this stress, and once one breaks, the remaining teeth are put under even more pressure. Change one or all worn or damaged sprockets immediately.

FREEWHEEL REMOVAL

Freewheel remover

FREEWHEEL TOOLS

Differences in freewheel tool design depend on the type of freewheel. To service a freewheel, you will need tools specific to it and your hub. Ask at a bike shop which tools you need.

1 FIT THE FREEWHEEL REMOVER

Remove the wheel nuts. Fit the freewheel remover over the axle and replace wheel nut or quick-release just tight enough to hold the remover in place.

2 LOOSEN OFF

Place the remover in a vice and turn the wheel anti-clockwise until the freewheel breaks free. Remove the axle nut and spin the remover and freewheel off the hub. Grease the hub threads when refitting.

Remover

Vice

Low ratio

High ratio

GEAR RATIOS

A gear, like a lever, is a means to change the rate at which work is done. The rate of change is called the ratio. On a bike the ratio is determined by the relative sizes of the crankset chainrings and the freewheel sprockets. With a 52-tooth (T) chainring, one complete turn of the cranks will rotate a wheel with a 13-T sprocket four times, a ratio of 4 to 1 (4:1). A 28-T chainring will turn a wheel with a 28-T sprocket once, a ratio of 1:1. A 52/13-T gear is big, and gives speed, while a 28/28-T gear is low, and gives the power to climb hills, albeit slowly.

Alternative Transmission Systems

THE MOST POPULAR ALTERNATIVE to the derailleur transmission system is the internal rear hub mechanism, which has a range of two, three, five and seven speeds. To change gear, a shift lever on the handlebars activates, via a cable, a control rod that passes through the hollow rear hub spindle. The mechanism needs little maintenance, apart from occasional lubrication and cable adjustment. Alternatives to the traditional chain transmission include belt and treadle drives (see glossary).

ROADSTER BIKE
Most utility bicycles, such as the roadster bike shown here, have traditionally used internal rear hub gear systems. Although hub gears are mechanically sophisticated, they are extremely dependable, and simple to use and service. Derailleur systems provide greater performance efficiency, but need more frequent servicing.

Gear shift lever

Transmission located inside rear hub

ANATOMY

Drum brake *Hub body* *Flange*

Axle/spindle *Gearing mechanism*

View hole

Control chain (attaches to cable)

Sprocket

THREE-SPEED REAR HUB TRANSMISSION
One advantage of internal rear hub mechanisms is that there are few damageable parts located on the outside of the bike. The system is virtually sealed, and allows the chain to be covered. Some mechanisms also incorporate a hub drum brake.

REAR HUB MECHANISM ADJUSTMENT (THREE-SPEED)

Chain guard

Adjuster

View hole (concealed)

1 CHECK CABLES
If there is any problem with the system, first check the cable and cable guides for stretching and damage, and adjust or replace as required.

2 LUBRICATE
If the mechanism has not been lubricated for some time, trickle drops of medium oil into it via the oiling nipple, and on to the control chain. Rotate cranks a few times in each gear.

3 ADJUST (3-SPEED)
Using the view hole, check the control rod and first link of the control chain exactly align when in second gear; if not, use the adjuster to align them.

LOOKING TO THE FUTURE
Developments in transmission technology include a computerized system that automatically changes gears in response to changes in pressure on the pedals and pedalling speed, both of which are monitored by sensors in the hub. When a pre-set range is exceeded, an electronic mechanism slides the rear sprocket to a new position and a new gear ratio.

BELT DRIVES
The quest for a lighter, cleaner, quieter, and lubrication-free alternative to the bicycle chain has resulted in many experiments with notched rubber belt drives, as on the *Twike* (above). Belt drives are already used on some folding bicycles.

TREADLE DRIVES
Treadle drives could become popular on Human Powered Vehicles (see glossary), since the driving motion is linear, not circular as with pedalling.

Bearings

ESSENTIALLY BEARINGS ACT as a support between two reciprocal mechanical parts (cup and cones) that rotate on each other. Made of stainless steel, bearings are precision-engineered to very accurate sizes. It is incredible how such small components can be so integrally important for the maximum efficiency of the bicycle. Indeed, bearings that are well greased and set for almost no resistance or play are vital for bike performance and speed. The ride and handling of a little-serviced bike improves dramatically once the main bearings (the headset and bottom bracket) and front and rear wheel hub bearings have been overhauled. Modern bearing components often feature sealed unit bearings for easy maintenance.

Lockring

Adjustable cup

Ball race

Ball race

Fixed cup

Axle/spindle

Pedal axle/spindle

Pedal body

PEDAL BEARINGS

It is vital to make sure your pedals are secure and the axles are straight. Also check and adjust your pedal bearings regularly for maximum energy efficiency. There are various types of pedal available, from traditional to step-in, or clipless, designs, which were originally developed from ski bindings.

BOTTOM BRACKET

To accommodate different frame and crank designs, bottom bracket axle lengths vary. Adjustable, cassette, and self-contained bottom bracket bearings need servicing more regularly if they are exposed to a lot of water, grit, and mud.

Toe clips

Toe straps

Pedal

Bottom bracket

Top headset
bearing assembly

Bottom headset
bearing assembly

Lock washer

Locknut

Top cone

Dust seals

Top
cup

Bottom cup

Ball races

HEADSETS

Headset assemblies are engineered by bicycle designers to endure a great amount of impact. Some modern designs incorporate roller bearings, which are cylindrical rather than spherical (ball) bearings, their advantage being that load is distributed over a greater surface area. However, most headsets still use conventional ball bearings, as they are far more economical to manufacture.

Axle/spindle

Freewheel body

Spoke flange

Hub body

Quick-release clamp

WHEEL HUBS

The shape of wheel hubs varies to some extent between manufacturers, but the basic components are the same. Hubs are available with adjustable bearings or replaceable cassette bearings, which are precision-machined for smoothness.

Spoke flange

Front hub

Headset

THE HEADSET HOLDS THE forks (steerer tube) in the head tube. Test for faults by lifting the front wheel off the ground and rotating the handlebars with one finger. They should move smoothly; if there are any grinding noises or the forks catch in certain positions, then the bearings need adjustment or regreasing. You should also test the headset for slack (below, right). Loose bearings must be corrected immediately, since stresses in the headset area are high, and a loose headset can self-destruct rapidly. You will need to use proper headset spanners; 32 mm spanners for most bikes; 36 mm for some mountain bikes. If the headset parts are alloy, take care not to bend them.

ANATOMY

Top bearing set

Locknut

Locknut washer

Adjustable top cup

Dust seal

Ball bearing race

Fixed top cone

Bottom bearing set

Fixed bottom cup

Ball bearing race

Dust seal

Fixed bottom cone

Top bearing set

HIGH STRESS ZONE
The head tube and headset have to tolerate a lot of impact stress within a relatively small area. It is not uncommon for the headset to work itself loose, so regular checks are advisable.

The head tube houses the forks, which in turn house the handlebar stem

Bottom bearing set

TESTING FOR SLACK
Firmly engage the front brake, then push the bike back and forth. A click-clunk sound indicates loose headset bearings or brake mounting bolts. Lift and lightly rotate the handlebars; roughness indicates over-tight bearings and/or that they need regreasing.

HEADSET ADJUSTMENT

Locknut

Top cup
spanner

Locknut
spanner

1 LOOSEN LOCKNUT

First make sure you have the correct
headset spanners; ill-fitting ones will damage
the locknut and may distort the bearing
surfaces. Loosen the locknut anti-clockwise.
(Locknuts with castellations rather than flat
edges can also be loosened with a small cold-
chisel.) Now slacken off the top cup – you
should be able to use your fingers.

2 ADJUST AND TIGHTEN TOP CUP

Gradually turn the top cup clockwise until
it is finger-tight against the bearings and there
is no play in the set. Reverse the cup ⅛–¼ turn,
and hold it in position with one of the headset
spanners. Then lock the cup in place by
carefully using a medium amount of clockwise
force with the other spanner, on the locknut.
Always work from an adjustment that is just
loose enough to avoid over-tightening the
bearings when you secure the locknut.

ANNUAL REBUILD

Headsets are exposed to stress, dirt, and
road shocks, so they should be stripped,
cleaned, and rebuilt at least once a year.

• Remove the handlebar stem (see p.15),
then the locknut and washer. Secure the
forks to the frame with string, or hold them
in place with one hand.

• Remove the adjustable top cup. If the
ball bearings are loose, most will stick to the
inside of the cup, so count them out. If they
are held in a race, simply lift it out. Slowly
draw the forks out of the head tube. If the
lower bearings are loose, gather them all
together and count them.

• Clean all parts in a biodegradable solvent
and wipe the fixed cones. Ball bearings must
be smooth and unpitted. Cones and cups
should be evenly coloured where the balls
run. Check the running grooves for
brinnelling (a series of small dents caused
by very hard impacts).

• Place the ball races on a glass surface to
see if they are bent or warped. If the headset
needs replacing, get a bike shop to do it.

Bearing race
in top cup

Ball
bearing

• Wash your hands thoroughly. This stops
the grease you use from getting contaminated.
Assuming all parts are in good condition,
lightly line the inside of the adjustable top
cup (pictured above) and fixed bottom cup
with a stiff, waterproof grease.

• Position the ball bearings and press
them right into the grease. Add sufficient
grease to coat each bearing. Be careful –
too much grease will leak, attract dirt, and
create a mess.

• Replace the forks and all other parts
carefully, so that no ball bearings dislodge.
Finally adjust as in Step 2, above.

Bottom Bracket

THE BOTTOM BRACKET axle, or spindle, rotates on bearings inside the bottom bracket shell. There are two common basic types of bottom bracket: adjustable (using cups and cones threaded into the bracket shell) and sealed cassette (where axle and bearings are a complete unit held in place within the bracket shell). Some cassettes are adjustable, most are not. Bottom brackets with adjustable bearings usually have a fixed cup (with no lockring) on the right-hand side, and an adjustable cup with holes and a lockring on the left-hand side. The bottom bracket axle and bearings should be cleaned and regreased at least once a year.

ANATOMY

Lockring

Adjustable cup

Ball race

Axle/spindle

Cone

Taper

Ball race

Fixed cup

BOTTOM BRACKET REMOVAL

1 REMOVE DUST-CAP
To adjust the bottom bracket, or strip it for cleaning and regreasing, the cranks must be removed. Take the dust-caps off; if they have smooth surfaces, they are press-fitted and can be prised off. If the caps have Allen key bolts or slots, unscrew them with the appropriate tool.

Crank mounting bolt

2 REMOVE CRANK BOLT
Once the dust-caps are off, undo and remove the crank mounting bolts, using a spanner or crank extractor. Ensure no washers are left inside. When you come to replace the crank bolts, make sure they are snug, but not too tight, as the threads may strip. (N.B. Crank bolts on new bikes need checking for tightness regularly.)

3 REMOVE CRANK WITH EXTRACTOR

Turn the inside bolt on the crank extractor anti-clockwise as far as it will go, then screw the extractor housing (which is threaded on the outside) firmly into the crank. Use a spanner if necessary. Turn the inside bolt clockwise until firm, but not too tight – if the crank is alloy, the threads may strip if forced. Remove the crank by tapping it with a wooden mallet. If it does not give, slowly increase the extractor tension, levering sharply when the crank starts to yield. Remove really stubborn cranks with a hammer and drift punch, or go to a bike shop.

4 TEST BEARINGS

Test bearings for excess play by pushing a crank to and fro firmly. A clicking sound indicates loose bearings. Lift the chain off the chainring and rest it on the bottom bracket. Spin the chainwheel; if it catches or runs roughly, the bearings are too tight and/or need regreasing

5 ADJUST BEARINGS

Make sure the fixed cup on the chainwheel side is tight; remove the crank arm and spider to get at it. This cup has a left-hand thread and is tightened anti-clockwise. On the non-chain side, turn the adjustable cup finger-tight against the bearings, then reverse it by ⅛ turn or so. Check bearings for play; a little is needed to compensate for tightening the lockring. Tighten lockring firmly with a lockring or pin spanner.

BOTTOM BRACKET CASSETTES

Sealed bottom bracket cassettes are relatively inexpensive, maintenance-free disposable units. They will usually last up to two years under normal use, or about a year under heavy use.

CASSETTE REMOVER

The *Shimano* hexagonal removing tool shown here is specifically designed to extract *Shimano* bottom bracket bearing cassettes.

FAG -TYPE CASSETTE

Above is a typical example, made by *FAG*, of a disposable, non-adjustable sealed bottom bracket cassette. The moulded shell, which holds the internal metal components in place, is constructed from a durable nylon plastic. One end of the cassette is detachable, to allow for fitting.

Hubs

CONVENTIONAL HUB BEARINGS (those with adjustable cones that allow the bearings to be removed, tightened, or loosened) should be checked regularly, adjusted, and cleaned and lubricated if necessary, for maximum wheel performance. This should be at the point where there is no resistance to the hub's rotation or any excess play. Cleaning and lubrication should be done more often if you ride a lot in wet and muddy conditions. More up-to-date cassette hub bearings should also be removed and replaced when necessary, but they are fairly durable and can last up to two years or more.

ANATOMY

 Locknut

 Washer

 Adjustable cone

 Ball bearings

CHECKING FOR BINDING
Remove the wheel, hold it directly in front of you, and spin it. If you feel any sticking or roughness as the wheel rotates, the bearings are too tight (binding), and the cones need adjusting.

Hub body

Ball bearings

Axle/spindle

CHECK FOR EXCESS PLAY
With the wheel in the rear dropouts and the axle nuts snug (tightening the axle nuts or a quick-release slightly tightens the bearings), push the wheel to and fro. If you feel any clicking, the bearings are loose (excess play) and the cones need adjusting.

Axle nuts snug in rear dropouts

HUB SERVICE AND ADJUSTMENT

1 REMOVE FREEWHEEL
Both screw-on or *Shimano* HyperGlide (cassette unit) freewheels must be removed (see p.55) before the rear hub bearing cones can be adjusted.

2 DISMANTLE HUB
Remove the locknuts, washers, cones, and the axle. Count the ball bearings as you remove them. Clean all parts in solvent and dry. Pack the hub cups with grease and press the ball bearings right into it.

3 ADJUST CONE
On wheels with freehubs, first make sure the right-side locknut and cone are secure. Using a pair of cone spanners, undo the left-side locknut and cone, taking care not to dislodge the bearings. Screw the cone tight against the bearings with your fingers, and reverse it by ⅛ turn or so. Now secure the cone with the locknut. Test again with the axle nuts or quick-release clamp in place. Readjust if needed.

CASSETTE BEARINGS
Cassette, or cartridge, bearings are the service-free answer to hub bearings. They are non-adjustable units made up of a cup, a cone, ball bearings, and grease. When play develops or the bearings are worn, the cartridges need replacing. Undo the grubscrews to remove the spacers and the axle. Then tap the cartridges out. Use thread adhesive to fix new cassettes in place, then replace the spacers and tighten the grubscrews.

Grubscrew

Front hub

Spacer

Bearing cartridge

Bearing cartridge

Spoke flange

Rear axle/spindle

Pedals

PEDALS CAN BE FITTED with either loose ball bearings held in place by an adjustable cone, or a self-contained cassette press-fitted into the pedal body. Some cassette bearings can be adjusted, others cannot. They can last for over two years or more without servicing, but if you do decide to service them you will need specialized tools. Many people do not bother; when their old pedals start creaking and grinding, they replace rather than repair them. Pedals with adjustable bearings should be cleaned and regreased every six months. The longevity of pedals depends on their quality; good ones will naturally last longer.

ANATOMY

Dust-cap

Locknut

Washer

Adjustable cone

Ball bearings

Toe straps

Toe clips

Crank

CHECKING A PEDAL
To check the pedal bearings, grasp the pedal with one hand and the crank with the other, then push the pedal back and forth. Clicking sounds indicate the bearings are loose. Spin the pedals. Any grinding and sticking means the bearings are too tight. If you use toe clips, check them for splits or cracks. Check the straps are in good condition, and that the buckles do not slip.

Pedal body

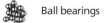
Ball bearings

REMOVING PEDALS
Remove both pedals from the cranks with a thin-jawed spanner, or, if the pedal axle threads are well greased, by unscrewing the sockets on the crank ends of the pedal axles with an Allen key. Remember the left-side pedal has a left-hand thread and should be unscrewed clockwise. Right-side pedals have normal right-hand threads and should be unscrewed anti-clockwise.

Left-side pedal axle thread

Axle/spindle

Fixed cone

Axle thread

SERVICING A PEDAL

1 REMOVE DUST-CAP

The purpose of dust-caps is to protect the pedal bearings from water and dirt. Remove the dust-cap to gain access to the locknut. Alloy dust-caps are threaded, so unscrew them with an adjustable spanner, or use a special tool if the dust-cap is unique. Sometimes plastic dust-caps are threaded as well, so try unscrewing them first. If that does not work, prise the dust-cap off with a thin screwdriver.

Dust-cap

Axle

Spanner

Locknut

2 DISMANTLE THE PEDAL

Hold the crank end of the pedal axle with a spanner, and unscrew the locknut and the adjustable cone. Shake out and count the ball bearings. Remove the axle, and shake out and count the ball bearings from the crank end. Clean all parts. Regrease the cups and press the ball bearings right into the grease. Replace the axle, and screw the cone in finger-tight. Replace the washer and the locknut. Spin the pedal to nest the bearings in place. Turn the cone flush against the bearings, then reverse it by ⅛ turn or so. Tighten the locknut, and check adjustment. Replace the dust-cap, grease the axle threads, and reinstall the pedal.

STEP-IN SYSTEM PEDALS

Step-in, or clipless, pedals work together with compatible cleats. When the rider steps into the pedal, a mechanism automatically grips on the cleat. The tension in this mechanism can be adjusted by a bolt located behind or underneath the pedal.

Adjustable cleat-grip mechanism

Spindle nut

Cartridge bearing

OFF-ROAD PEDALS

Double-sided pedals like the *Shimano* SPD (right) are specially designed for off-road use. Compatible shoes have recessed clips, so the rider can walk or run freely if necessary.

Cleat tension bolts

COMPONENTS

Step-in pedal axles use sealed cartridge bearings. If a pedal rattles, the spindle nut or bearing cartridge may be loose.

Routine Maintenance

BIKES ARE MACHINES, AND PERFORM best when well tuned and looked after. This every rider can provide for his or her bike by way of routine maintenance, which includes keeping the bike clean, lubricated, and regularly serviced. The more time that is spent with the bike, understanding how it works, the more instinctive and intuitive its rider will become to real and potential problems. Essentially, routine maintenance is a preventative measure: you will get better at avoiding problems by examining the bike closely and knowing its exact mechanical condition. The equation is quite simple: the more familiar you are with your bike, the better it will feel and perform.

HOME BIKE MECHANIC

Becoming an able bike mechanic is very satisfying, but it may take a little time. Don't be over-ambitious, and don't be afraid to visit your local bike shop if you need advice or professional assistance.

CLEANING

For cleaning your bike, use a selection of long-handled brushes. Toothbrushes are especially good for reaching awkward intricate parts. Use cloths to wipe away grease and for drying the bike. Thorough cleaning is vital – accumulated dirt is abrasive, and increases wear on parts. So a clean bike makes good economical sense too.

Assorted cleaning equipment

Pro-quality grease gun and cartridge

LUBRICATION

Keep your bike regularly lubricated for good performance and durability. Lubrication reduces friction, prevents parts from grinding or fusing together, and protects against rust. Also, lubricate your bike whenever you clean it.

Cleaning

SERVICING A BIKE can be made a much more satisfactory and pleasant task once the bike has been cleaned thoroughly. Cleaning makes bike parts easier to get at and handle, and you will be able to identify mechanical problems more readily. Grime, especially mud and dust, contains tiny particles that are highly abrasive, so regular cleaning following a ride will also help maintain your bike parts in good condition and make them last longer. It is best to develop a methodical approach to a full-scale wash, keeping your hands as clean as possible at every stage, otherwise you will simply transfer grime from one bit of the bike to another. If your bike does not need a full-scale wash, wipe it down with a damp cloth. Always dry and lubricate your bike after washing to avoid rust.

JET-SPRAY WASH
If your bike is very heavily mud-encrusted, which is only likely to be the case if it is a mountain bike, wash it thoroughly with a high-pressure jet-spray hose. Jet-spray hoses are powerful enough to take off transfers, and even paint in some cases, so take care not to stand too close to the bike. Avoid spraying water directly at the bearings, which are sensitive.

SOAPY WASH
For a soapy wash to remove all greasy grime, use a bucket of suds, brushes, and sponges. Help preserve the environment and the bike's wax finish by using a low-alkaline soap or washing-up liquid, or otherwise a biodegradable cleaner such as *Bike Elixir Wash & Wax*. Start by washing the frame, then move on to more intricate parts of the bike.

Long-handled kitchen brush

DETAILED SCRUB

Remember to scrub the rims and tyres thoroughly (left), removing any grime that may hamper braking efficiency. Use the brush to get into cavities around the gear mechanisms (above), and all other nooks and crannies where dirt collects. Rinse all parts with clean water.

BIKE-SPECIFIC EQUIPMENT

To clean intricate parts of the bike, such as the chain, specialist cleaning equipment is available from bike shops. However, you can still clean a dirty chain by breaking it and soaking it in a solvent to remove excess grease before washing it with a regular brush. After washing, use a wire brush to remove any stubborn grease. Dry the chain in an oven before relubricating.

FREEWHEEL BRUSH

Freewheels are notoriously difficult to clean, so use a stiff plastic freewheel brush (above) to reach accumulated grease, mud, and grass between the sprockets.

CHAIN BRUSH-BATH

An effective way to clean the chain is to use a brush-bath, such as the *Park Chain Bath* (left). After attaching the bath to the chain, hold it while you turn the cranks. Brush-baths work best if the solvent and the chain lubricant are from the same manufacturer.

Lubrication

THE TRADITIONAL LUBRICANT, petroleum oil, works well when first applied, but it soon attracts abrasive dirt and has poor resistance to washing away by water. Bikes lubricated with oil need frequent cleaning and relubricating. A far better choice are bike-specific modern lubricants with synthetic ingredients that greatly increase durability and water-resistance (such as *Finish Line*, *Superspray*, and *Pedros Synlube*). Always use a lubricant sparingly and with precision; too much lubricant or grease will attract dirt and increase wear on the parts. Always wipe away any excess, and dry the bike thoroughly when you finish. Greases can be either petroleum-based, or synthetic lubricants mixed with a thickener and other performance-enhancing additives. Whatever grease you use, never mix them, as incompatible additives can render the lubricant useless.

MEDIUM-WEIGHT LUBRICANT
Use a medium-weight lubricant for bushings (see glossary), which are usually made of brass and include the pivot point pins in the front derailleur and rear derailleur (left), jockey wheels, and any springs holding components in tension. It is important to stop dirt penetrating bushings, as it will cause corrosion and reduce efficiency. Use the container nozzle to trickle the lubricant directly into the part, and wipe away any excess.

LIGHT-WEIGHT LUBRICANT
Use a light- or medium-weight lubricant for the chain and freewheel sprockets, and to lubricate threads when reassembling components. The quickest and most convenient way to apply a light lubricant is in aerosol spray form. To lubricate the chain (right), simply spin the cranks backwards and direct the spray at the moving chain. Wipe off any excess from the outside link plates until they are almost dry to the touch. Also direct the spray at the freewheel sprockets while the chain is moving.

Seat post

Seat tube

SEAT POST LUBRICATION

Remove the seat post (left), then apply grease liberally to the outside of the post before replacing it inside the seat tube. This is extremely important, as the grease prevents the seat post, which is made of aluminium, from fusing with the seat tube, which is in most cases steel. If the components do become fused, it is virtually impossible to separate them. This procedure should be carried out annually. Do the same to the handlebar stem before replacing it in the steerer tube.

BEARINGS

Use grease to relubricate the bearings (the headset, the bottom bracket, and the hubs) after you have dismantled them, cleaned all parts in a solvent, and removed all traces of old grease. A pro-qualtiy grease gun (right) is excellent for the job. Press the ball bearings right into the grease.

Grease gun

Nozzle

Spring-tensioned lever

Cable guide

CABLE LUBRICATION

Use grease to lubricate cables (but not *Teflon*-lined cables) inside cable housing. If your bike does not have slotted cable guides (left), which allow sections of cable housing to slide along the wire, unthread the wire and cable housing completely, then grease and rethread them.

DIY GREASE GUN

A cheap and equally effective alternative to using a pro-quality grease gun is to improvise and make your own. Buy a plastic wide-bore hypodermic syringe (available at most chemists), remove the needle if there is one, then fill the syringe with grease. Control the flow of grease using the plunger.

Syringe

Grease

Preparing for a Ride

EVEN IF YOU ARE RELATIVELY FIT and your bike is in top-notch condition, problems can still arise. You should be prepared for all eventualities by carrying a contingency tool kit, a basic first aid kit, and if you are touring long-distance, various specialist items as well. In addition, make sure you take the right clothes; wear layers that you can remove or put on as the weather changes. A helmet is also highly recommended.

Bandage

Zinc oxide plaster

Plasters

Safety pins

Scissors

Lint

Antiseptic cream

Frame pump

Multi-tool

Four-inch adjustable spanner

Tyre lever

Puncture repair kit

Roll of electrical tape

Assorted nuts and bolts

BASIC FIRST AID KIT
Carry a basic first aid kit even if you are not venturing far from civilization. Injuries should always be treated immediately, and medical help sought as quickly as possible, if needed.

CONTINGENCY TOOL KIT
Always carry a contingency tool kit for roadside repairs, as well as a pump. The kit should be small and light, so it can easily fit into a pocket or saddle pouch.

CO₂ CANISTERS
For those keen on "superlite" cycling, CO$_2$ canisters can be used instead of a pump. Canisters act fast (two seconds), making them great for racing and in bad weather. They are not suited to long-distance touring, due to the finite number that can be carried.

Canister and connector nozzle

TOURING

Specialist touring bikes are available, but most bikes, except some road-racing machines, can be adapted to touring use. However, in terms of sheer versatility, mountain bikes are hard to beat for touring, on- and off-road. The *F.W. Evans* heavy-duty tourer pictured here is a modern mountain bike designed for comfort, stability, and load-carrying. The bike's frame geometry is carefully calculated to minimize the effect of carrying heavy front and rear panniers over long distances.

Good-quality helmet is essential for all riding

Standard pannier bags hook over top of rear pannier rack

Low-slung front racks centre pannier bags over front hub axle for optimum steering performance

Heavy-duty touring bike

Waterbottle and cage

Front mudguard and pannier rack

Front pannier

Rear pannier

Rear mudguard and pannier rack

TOURING ACCESSORIES

• Waterbottles: carry as many as your bike frame will permit. Dehydration can become a serious problem if you are cycling continuously.

• Mudguards: they might appear old-fashioned, but you will be very grateful for them if you are riding for more than a day at a time in the wet. Having a sodden behind can be very miserable!

• Quality panniers: invest in panniers that are strong, water-resistant and durable. Also make sure that they can easily be taken off the racks when you leave the bike.

• Pannier racks: use racks that keep the panniers well out of the wheels. Avoid getting stranded by always carrying spare mounting bolts or clips, as heavy loads can sheer them.

Pre-ride Check Drill

BEFORE ANY LONG-DISTANCE ride, a good, systematic check of your entire bike is essential. If the bike is sound, this can be done very quickly. Naturally it will take longer if you discover a problem – and it is best to sort it out now, otherwise you could end up in a real mess later. With practice, you will instinctively know where to start looking for the cause of the problem if something looks, sounds, or feels odd as you are checking.

• FRAME AND FORKS

Check frame alignment, and all the tubes for dents and scratches. Examine the forks, checking the underside of the down tube where it meets the head tube. Fractured paint on a steel frame may be a sign of structural failure. A discoloured ring on bonded aluminium or composite frames could be caused by glue failure.

• CABLES

Check that all cable housing is sound, the cables are not kinked or frayed, and that they move easily and do not slip. Tighten the cable anchor bolts just enough to start denting the wire.

• RIMS

Check for trueness: hold a tool near the rim and spin the wheel. More than 3 mm (⅛ in) lateral or vertical movement calls for trueing. Ensure the rims are clean and not dented.

• TYRES

Check the tyre pressure, the tread for wear, and the tyre walls for cuts, embedded gravel, or glass.

• SPOKES

Test for bends or breaks, and ensure the spokes are evenly tight. On the rear wheel, the spokes near the freewheel should be less tight than those on the opposite side.

• BEARINGS

Check bottom bracket bearings for excess play or binding, and adjust if necessary. Check wheel hub bearings, and tighten axle nuts or quick-release levers. Check headset bearings, and tighten if needed. Check pedal bearings.

• SEAT POST AND SADDLE

Tighten seat post bolt firmly. Tighten saddle clamp securely. This bolt sometimes feels tight when in fact it is still loose; check by trying to move the saddle.

• STEM BOLT

Tighten firmly. The bolt should be tight enough to stay in place when riding, but move if the bike takes a fall. To test, hold the front wheel with your knees and twist the handlebars. Also tighten handlebar binder bolt firmly.

TYRE PRESSURES

Inflate tyres to the correct pressure. Under-inflated tyres increase rolling resistance and puncture risk. The pressure listed on the tyre wall is only a reference point calculated by inflating the tyre to twice that pressure without blowing it off the rim. Optimum tyre pressure varies according to weight and conditions; experiment, as 34.5–69 kPa (5–10 lbf/in^2) can affect performance.

• BRAKE LEVERS AND MOUNTS

Tighten mounting bolts firmly. Levers should be tight enough to stay in place when riding, but move in a crash. If a lever feels loose/too tight, adjust the lever pivot bolt.

• BRAKE BLOCK BOLTS

Tighten the mounting bolts firmly. Check the brake blocks accurately meet the rim, with the correct amount of toe-in.

• FREEWHEEL

You should hear a healthy, even, and rapid clicking sound from the freewheel when coasting. Sprocket teeth must not be chipped or bent. Test for damaged teeth by turning the cranks hard in each gear.

• REAR DERAILLEUR

Tighten mounting bolt firmly. Check rear derailleur cable and operate gears to check shifting accuracy and, if included, the indexing adjustment. Adjust if necessary. Tighten pulley bolts firmly.

• CHAIN AND CHAINRINGS

Pedal backwards, watching the derailleur rollers for any frozen links. Lubricate if necessary. Check for wear. Check chainrings are true and teeth are not chipped or bent. Tighten chainring mounting bolts firmly.

• FRONT DERAILLEUR

Operate gears to check high/low (side-to-side) travel. Tighten the derailleur mounting bolt and the cable anchor bolt firmly.

• CRANK BOLTS

Test for tightness. Tighten steel bolts firmly. For alloy bolts, first use a steel bolt and tighten firmly, then replace the alloy bolt snugly.

Monthly Service Chart

FOR A WELL TUNED BIKE, a monthly service is highly recommended. This consists largely of simple checks for wear, and light lubrication and adjustment. Have all your cleaning equipment, lubricants, and tools at hand, so that if you do discover a problem, it can be dealt with immediately and efficiently. Be methodical and thorough in your approach, and service the bike's components in logical groups. Start by giving the bike a general clean, which will make it less messy and very much more pleasant to work on.

BRAKES
- Check brake blocks for wear. Remove any embedded grit.
- Check blocks meet the rims accurately, and toe-in is correct.
- Check brake block mounting bolts.
- Check brake lever mounting bolts.
- Lubricate brake pivot bolts, and tighten as necessary.

CABLES
- Inspect all cable housing for damage. Replace if necessary.
- Clean and examine all cable wires for kinks and frays. Replace if necessary.
- Check for cable stretch or slipping by operating parts concerned (brakes and gears). Compensate for stretching by adjusting barrel adjusters and/or cable anchor bolts.

WHEELS
- Check rims for trueness and even spoke tension. More than 3 mm (⅛ in) lateral or vertical movement requires trueing.
- Clean rims and check they are not dented or dimpled.
- Check each spoke for bends or breaks. Replace if necessary.

TYRES AND TUBES
- Check tyre pressure is correct.
- Clean the tyres and inspect tyre treads for wear.
- Remove any embedded gravel or glass from tread or tyre walls.
- Replace over-repaired inner tubes or any with slow punctures.

CHAIN
- Check chain is not excessively worn or stretched.
- Check chain for frozen links.
- Lubricate with chain lubricant.

CHAINSET AND FREEWHEEL

- Clean chainrings; check they are true, and check for worn or broken teeth.
- Check crank arms are tight on bottom bracket axle.
- Clean and lubricate freewheel, and check for wear.
- Check freewheel sprockets for worn or broken teeth.

DERAILLEURS

- Check the side-to-side travel of rear and front derailleurs, and adjust travel adjuster screws if necessary.
- Clean derailleur cages, and lubricate all pivot points and bushings.
- Check indexing accuracy and adjust cable tension at barrel adjusters and/or cable anchor bolts as required.

HEADSET

- Check headset bearings for excess play or binding. Make any necessary tightening or loosening adjustments.
- Lubricate headset if grease is broken down or contaminated with dirt.

BOTTOM BRACKET

- Test bottom bracket bearings for excess play or binding. If you have adjustable cup-and-cone bearings, tighten or loosen if necessary.

HUBS

- Check front and rear hub bearings for excess play or binding. If you have adjustable cup-and-cone bearings, tighten or loosen if necessary.
- Tighten hub axle nuts and quick-release levers.

PEDALS

- Check pedal bodies are not cracked.
- If pedals are loose, tighten the mounting bolts firmly.
- Inspect toe clips for damage, and toe straps for fraying. Make sure the buckles cannot slip.
- Check pedal bearings and adjust if necessary.

GENERAL

- Apply wax or polish if necessary.
- Check frame alignment and all the tubes for dents or damage.
- Check every bolt and nut is secure, even if you have used thread adhesive. Tighten bolts with the right tools, and with caution; alloy bike parts can be damaged by over-tightening.

Annual Service Chart

ONCE A YEAR, YOUR BIKE should be completely overhauled. This involves stripping down all the components, cleaning, replacing parts when necessary, relubricating, and reassembly. Some components, such as bottom brackets and hub bearings, may require specialized tools available only at a bike shop, but the majority of these tasks can be accomplished using simple tools. One good trick is to break down complete overhauls and integrate them into your monthly service: pedals one month, brakes the next, then derailleurs, and so on.

BRAKES
- Lubricate brake pivot bolts and bushings.
- Strip down and clean front and rear brakes, and brake levers.
- Replace brake blocks if necessary.
- Reassemble brakes, checking blocks meet the rims accurately and toe-in is correct.

CABLES
- Dismantle all cables. Replace damaged cable housing or frayed or kinked cable wires.
- Grease cables inside cable housing and reassemble, but do not grease *Teflon*-lined cables. Tighten cable anchor bolts just enough to dent the wire, and fine-tune using the barrel adjusters. Test cable tension by operating parts.

WHEELS
- Check rims for trueness and even spoke tension. More than 3 mm (⅛ in) lateral or vertical movement requires trueing.
- Clean rims. Replace any that are dented or beyond repair.
- Check each spoke for bends or breaks. Replace if necessary.
- Take wheels to a bike shop to be trued if necessary.

TYRES AND TUBES
- Remove any embedded gravel or glass from tread or tyre walls.
- Replace tyres with excessively worn treads or tyre walls.
- Replace over-repaired inner tubes or any with slow punctures.
- Check tyre pressure is correct.

CHAIN
- Replace chain if it is excessively worn.
- Check chain for frozen links.
- Break and remove chain, and soak it in solvent to clean. Alternatively, use a chain brush-bath. Replace chain and lubricate with chain lubricant.

CHAINSET AND FREEWHEEL

- Check chainrings and freewheel sprockets for wear. If replacement is required, replace all chainrings, freewheel sprockets, and the chain together.
- Check crank arms are tight on bottom bracket axle and not cracked.
- Check freewheel operates smoothly. If it sticks or sounds rough, replace it. Lubricate.

DERAILLEURS

- Disassemble front and rear derailleur bodies and cages, clean all parts and relubricate. Replace worn jockey wheels.
- Reassemble, adjusting side-to-side travel and position of derailleurs in each gear position correctly.

HEADSET

- Disassemble upper and lower parts of the headset, clean all parts. Replace and grease ball bearings.
- Reassemble and check adjustment.

BOTTOM BRACKET

- Disassemble bottom bracket, clean all parts, replace and grease ball bearings. Replace worn-out cassette bearings.

HUBS

- Strip down front and rear hub bearings, clean all parts, replace and grease ball bearings. Replace worn-out cassette bearings.
- Tighten hub axle nuts and quick-release levers.

PEDALS

- Replace cracked pedal bodies.
- Disassemble pedal bearings, clean all parts, replace and grease ball bearings.
- Replace damaged toe clips or frayed straps.
- For step-in pedals, clean and relubricate step-in mechanism, and check tension setting.

GENERAL

- Check frame alignment and all the tubes for dents and damage.
- Remove and regrease seat post and handlebar stem to avoid parts fusing.
- Wax frame and components (but not wheel rims).

Emergency Repairs

IT'S THE MOMENT ANY cyclist dreads: you are out on a ride and one vital piece of equipment breaks without warning. If you are out in the wild on a mountain bike, you could be in a real mess. Try a little ingenuity – the solution may be closer than you realize. In fact the list of quick fixes for bike emergencies is endless. All they require is a little imagination: most things can be fixed by improvising with objects to hand.

• BANDAGED SADDLE
If the saddle padding is shot, wrap a shirt or sweater around the seat and secure it with a piece of string.

• LOST GEAR
For a broken derailleur, leave the chain on a middle cog and strap the derailleur with a cord to keep the jockey arm extended and the chain taut.

• TYRES
If your progress is being hampered by a slow puncture, remove the inner tube carefully from the tyre, then wrap some electrical tape around the leaky spot.

• BROKEN CHAIN
If a link pin disappears, insert a twig or wire through the link holes, and bind it with tape or cloth. Expect to rebind it every half-hour or so, but it will keep you going.

• PATCHED PEDAL
If a pedal body shatters but the axle survives, rebuild it with wire, or make a substitute pedal out of wood. If the axle breaks, lash a piece of wood to the side of the crank.

• Split Saddle

When a saddle splits down to its frame, the choice is between riding standing up or fixing it. If there is any padding left, bandage the saddle with cloth and tie it.

• Front Derailleur

If it breaks, remove the cable and the mechanism, and move the chain to the middle chainwheel.

• Brake Lever

If one of your brake levers snaps, force a short, hollow piece of plastic tube over the remaining lever stump, and secure it with some tape.

• Headset Bearings

If conditions are muddy or you ride through a stream, protect the bearings by sliding a section of split tube around the base of the head tube.

• Snapped Straddle Wire

The straddle wire and any sections of brake cable wire that are not threaded through cable housing can be replaced with taut lengths of string if they get frayed or break.

• Stuff It

Every cyclist should carry a pump, but the odds are that you will be without one when you need it most. Artificially reinflate the tyre by filling it with grass or leaves, thin flexible branches, or even old newspapers.

• Temporary Patches

Modern skinwall tyres are thin, and if the casing gets badly gashed, it can leave a hole big enough to let an inflated tube bulge through. The trick is to line the hole with some thin material: bits of cardboard, old inner tube, tree bark, even gum wrappers. Then reinsert and inflate the tube.

• Cables

If you damage the cable housing channel on a gear lever and the cable flops out when you use it, wrap a plastic tie around the housing to keep it in the channel. Plastic ties can also be used to hold components in position.

HOMEMADE TOOL

To improvise a spanner, tie a length of string (or wire) to a flat-sided stick. Wrap the string around the nut or part you want to move; wind the string clockwise to tighten, anti-clockwise to release. Brace the end of the stick against the nut, and use the long end as a spanner handle.

Flat-sided stick

String

Gear shifter

Zip tie

PLASTIC TIES

Always keep a supply of plastic ties; they are strong and very useful, especially for attaching parts to the bike frame where mounting bolts have snapped or been lost. Plastic ties can be stored in numerous places on a bike: taped to the saddle rails or to a pannier strut, or concealed inside the seat post.

CABLE MENDS

Broken cables can be rejoined by tying each end to another object, such as a stick, an old tin can, or a length of rag or shoelace. If you cannot rejoin the cable because it has snapped close to the control lever, improvise another means of operating the part by hooking and pulling it over a waterbottle bolt on the frame, or some other handy item.

Broken cable

Hole for attaching cable

Coat hanger wire

Rivet

Chain link

WIRE CHAIN RIVET

If you snap a chain and lose the rivet, a piece of wire can hold the links in place. The kind of wire used to make coat hangers is ideal. Run the chain on a rear cog large enough to keep the chain clear of the other cogs, or else the wire may get caught in the space between the cogs. Insert the wire into the empty rivet hole, then cut the wire, leaving 2.5 cm (1 in) or so sticking out each side. Bend the ends backwards along the chain, and bind them into place with tape.

Washer

Threads cut by axle

Crank arm

Improvised wooden crank bolt

WOODEN BOLT

Use a pocket knife – no off-road rider should be without one – to carve temporary replacements for bolts and other parts out of wood. Use the hardest bit of wood you can find. The wooden crank bolt (above) was made slightly too large, so that the bottom bracket axle would cut threads in it when inserted, making it more secure. Wooden bolts are of course limited in strength, but they should get you home.

Solid post

Buckled rim

POTATO CHIP STOMP

After a collision or "wipe-out", any rider can end up with a badly buckled wheel, usually in the shape of a potato chip. Remedy the problem by removing the wheel and holding it with the sections curving away from you at the top and bottom. Place the wheel at an angle against a tree, post, or any solid object. Brace the bottom of the wheel with your foot, grasp the sides curving towards you at three and nine o'clock, and push against them firmly until the rim is straight enough to fit the wheel back on the bike. Use a spoke key to tighten the spokes and true the wheel as best you can. If you do not have a spoke key or adjustable spanner, remove the tyre and adjust the spoke nipples with a screwdriver. Ride home very slowly.

Frame Damage

DAMAGE TO A BICYCLE FRAME can either be the result of shock impacts, or simply old age and metal fatigue, or a combination of both. Much frame damage is the result of cumulative stresses, so it is important to check for damage as part of your regular servicing, as well as after any serious knocks. Some apparently minor "injuries" can induce much more serious failure later, so pay attention to all frame damage, at least until you have had the bike checked by a qualified frame-builder. You will not necessarily see any cracked paint or crumpled tubes when a frame is damaged, but inaccurate steering is a sure sign. Steel-framed bikes are the simplest to repair, as tubes can be removed and replaced relatively easily and without significant structural consequences. Glued aluminium frames are also easy to repair, in contrast to those that are welded, since reheating the previously heat-treated structure is likely to upset the metal's composition.

Rear dropouts

Head tube

String

Seat tube

Taut string

CHECK ALIGNMENT
Peculiar steering is often a result of a bent frame throwing the wheels out of track. To check tracking, attach a length of string to a rear dropout, wrap it once around the head tube about half way up, then tie it to the other rear dropout. Make sure the string is taut. Measure the distance from the seat tube to the string on each side with a ruler. Ideally the distances should be identical, but most production bikes are generally off-track by up to 3 mm (⅛ in). Over 3 mm (⅛ in) difference between the two sides indicates a bent frame. Take the bike to a shop for professional realignment.

Chain stay

Bottom bracket

Bent hanger

BENT REAR DERAILLEUR HANGER

This can be caused by the rear derailleur hitting the ground or snagging the wheel (due to poor side-to-side travel adjustment: see p.46). This can seriously foul gearing performance, particularly on indexed-shift systems. Steel frames can usually be bent back into shape by a professional; aluminium tends to snap if this is attempted, requiring a welding job. Some aluminium frames have replaceable hangers.

Lug

Crack

Damage to top tube

FRONTAL IMPACT

A serious front-on crash may not bend the front forks at all. On the frame shown here, the forks, which are relatively strong, have survived, but the shock of the impact has been transmitted to the now crumpled top and down tubes. This kind of damage is not irreparable, but worth the expense only if the frame is fairly valuable.

Damage to down tube

FRAME CRACKS

These generally tend to appear around frame joints, and are a consequence of extreme old age or uneven heating during construction. Steel tubes can be replaced individually if the frame has lugs. A minor crack can be brazed-over to stop it spreading.

OTHER DAMAGE

The only damage likely to cause serious injury is total tube separation – thankfully very rare. Look out for bent forks and cracked seat lugs or joints, which can be dangerous and should be repaired at a bike shop. Stripped bottom bracket threads can be recut at a bike shop too.

STUNT RIDING

Mountain bikes encourage "bunny-hopping" jumps and other stunts that are potentially frame-damaging. Skilled riders absorb impact with their arms and legs, leaving the bike intact. However, without these skills, repeated abuse of this kind will eventually take its toll on the bike frame, and most manufacturers' warranties will not cover it.

Troubleshooting Chart

A BICYCLE IS A DYNAMIC extension of your body. Learn to tune into your bike, so that you automatically listen to it and watch it as you cycle along. The better you ride, the more aware you will become of the bike's mechanical condition. All bikes produce a constant melody of whirs, clicks, and soft hisses that form a rhythmic pattern when all is working well. Listen, look, and feel for unusual noises and riding sensations, and try to track down the source immediately. Use this chart as a rough guide to getting to the root of a problem.

SYMPTOM	LIKELY CAUSE	SOLUTION	PAGE
Knocking or jittering when brakes applied	• Brakes out of adjustment • Forks loose in head tube • Bulge in rim or rim out of true • Brake mounting bolts loose	• Centre brakes and/or adjust brake block toe-in • Tighten headset • True wheel or take rim to a bike shop for repair • Tighten bolts	• 24–25 • 60–61 • 32–33 • 25
Brakes do not work effectively	• Brake cables are sticking/ stretched/damaged • Brake blocks worn down • Brake blocks/rim greasy, wet, or dirty • Brakes out of adjustment • Brake levers are binding	• Clean/adjust/regrease/ replace cables • Replace blocks • Clean blocks and rim • Centre brakes • Adjust brake levers	• 22–23 • 24 • 25 • 23, 26
Brakes squeak or squeal when applied	• Brake blocks/rim dirty or wet • Brake blocks worn down • Brake block toe-in incorrect • Brake arms loose	• Clean blocks and rim • Replace blocks • Correct block toe-in • Tighten mounting bolts	 • 25 • 24 • 25
Frequent punctures	• Tyre pressure too low • Spoke protruding into rim • Tyre not checked after previous puncture • Tyre tread/casing worn • Inner tube old or faulty • Tyre unsuited to rim	• Correct tyre pressure • File down spoke • Remove sharp object embedded in tyre • Replace tyre • Replace inner tube • Replace with correct tyre	 • 31 • 34–35 • 34–35 • 34–35
Inaccurate steering	• Headset loose or binding • Front forks bent • Wheels not aligned	• Adjust/tighten headset • Take bike to a bike shop for frame realignment • Check tracking and align wheels	• 60–61 • 32

Symptom	Likely Cause	Solution	Page
Wheel wobbles	• Hub cones loose • Wheel out of true • Headset binding	• Adjust hub bearings • True wheel • Adjust headset	• 64–65 • 32–33 • 60–61
Clicking noises when pedalling	• Loose bottom bracket axle/bearings • Loose pedal axle/bearings • Stiff chain link • Loose crankset • Bent bottom bracket/pedal axle	• Adjust bottom bracket • Adjust bearings/axle nut • Lubricate chain • Tighten crank bolts • Replace axle	• 62–63 • 66–67 • 40–43 • 52 • 62–63/ 66–67
Grinding noises when pedalling	• Bottom bracket bearings too tight • Pedal bearings too tight • Chain fouling derailleurs • Derailleur pulleys dirty/binding	• Adjust bearings • Adjust bearings • Adjust chain line • Clean and lubricate pulleys	• 62–63 • 66–67 • 40–43 • 47
Chain jumps off freewheel sprocket or chainring	• Chainring loose • Chainring out of true • Rear or front derailleur side-to-side travel out of adjustment • Chainring teeth bent or broken	• Tighten mounting bolts • True if possible, or replace • Adjust derailleur travel • Repair or replace chainring/set	• 53 • 52 • 46, 51 • 52–53
Chain slips	• Chain worn/stretched • Stiff link in chain • Chainring or freewheel sprocket teeth excessively worn/chipped • Chain/chainring/freewheel not compatible	• Replace chain • Lubricate or replace link • Replace chainring, sprockets, and chain • Seek advice at a bike shop	• 40–43 • 40–43 • 53, 55, 41–43
Gear shifts faulty	• Front or rear derailleur not adjusted properly • Derailleur cables sticking/stretched/damaged • Indexed shifting not adjusted properly	• Adjust derailleurs • Lubricate/tighten/replace cables • Adjust indexing	• 50–51/ 46–49 • 44–45 • 48–49
Freewheel does not freewheel	• Pawls (see glossary) are jammed	• Lubricate. If problem persists, replace freewheel	• 55

Glossary

A

Aerodynamic drag The resistance of air to the movement of an object; the combination of a) pressure drag – the resistance from low pressure zones behind a shape, and b) friction drag – when the layer of air next to the surface of a vehicle separates from it.

Airfoil (aerofoil) A structure that has a streamlined profile to reduce drag.

B

Barrel adjuster Barrel-shaped knobs through which cables pass – used to fine-tune the adjustment of cables to take up or give slack; can be turned clockwise or anti-clockwise. Barrel adjusters are located on the brake levers, gear shifters, and front and rear derailleurs.

Bearing cartridge/cassette Sealed unit containing lubricated ball or roller bearings. Disposable and virtually maintenance-free, cassettes can be fitted to the bottom bracket, hubs, and pedals.

Belt drive Friction-grip belt, sometimes with notches for added grip. Clean, but inefficient and expensive.

Bosses Brazed-on mounting points on a bike frame for bolting on items such as cantilever brakes, down-tube gear levers, and pannier racks.

Bottom bracket shell The part of a bicycle frame that accommodates the bottom bracket bearings (adjustable components or a sealed unit) and axle, on to which the cranks are threaded. The shell is threaded on the inside.

Brake block Rubber or synthetic shoe that engages with the braking surface of the wheel rim to stop the bicycle.

Brazing Process of joining two pieces of steel tubing together using a non-ferrous alloy such as brass, which has a lower melting point than the metals being joined.

Bushing A sleeve or tube on which a part, or parts, rotate.

C

Cable guide Brazed-on or riveted to the bike frame, cable guides keep cables in position as they pass along the tubes and prevent them fouling the rider's body or any other parts of the bike.

Cadence Pedalling rate, measured as the number of crank rotations per minute. Tourers and commuters pedal at 55–85 rpm, racers from 95–130 rpm, depending on conditions.

Caliper brake Consists of two hinged arms. Pulling the brake cable activates a pincer-like movement, forcing the brake blocks to engage the wheel rim.

Cantilever brake Consists of two separate brake arms that pivot on bosses brazed on to the frame. A straddle wire connects both arms, and cable tension is centred at the straddle yoke, so both arms are activated simultaneously.

Chainset Collective term for the cranks and the chainrings.

Cleat A device for locking a shoe and pedal together. A cleat is a small plastic or metal plate that is permanently attached to the sole of a shoe. The cleat is designed to engage positively with the pedal.

Crank Lever arm joining the pedal to the chainwheel and bottom bracket.

D

Down tube The tube that connects the head tube to the bottom bracket.

Drag See *Aerodynamic drag*.

Dropouts Slots at the front and rear of the bike for holding the wheel axles.

Drum brake See *Hub brake*.

F

Ferrule Alloy component that fits on the end of a section of cable housing to prevent the housing becoming frayed when secured in a cable stop brazed on to the frame.

Flange Circular collar projecting from each side of a wheel hub, with eyelets into which the spoke ends are secured.

Frame set All the tubes that make up the frame of a bicycle.

Front derailleur Front transmission mechanism (generally cable-activated) that guides the chain up or down between the inner and outer chainrings.

G

Gauge Thickness or diameter.

Gear ratio Amount of motion or work per amount of motion or work. On a bicycle, one rotation of a chainring with 48 teeth will cause a wheel with a sprocket of 12 teeth to rotate 4 times: a gear ratio of 4:1.

Groupset A typical groupset includes the following components: chainset, freewheel, hubs, gear shifters and derailleurs, brake levers and brake mechanisms, and bottom bracket axle.

H

Headset Divided into two parts at the top and bottom of the head tube, the headset contains the bearings on which the steering tube rotates.

Head tube Tube in which the steering tube rotates by means of the headset bearings. The head tube angle can have an affect on steering performance.

HPV Human Powered Vehicle. Technically, a bicycle is an HPV. In practice, the term is used for any human powered vehicle that is not a bicycle.

Hub brake A drum and shoe device, which brakes the wheel at the hub as opposed to the rim.

Hybrid Term given to a street bike design that fuses together key features of a mountain bike and a tourer: straight handlebars, bar-mounted brake and gear levers, cantilever brakes, and wheels with narrow-section multi-purpose tyres.

I

Indexed shifting Cable-activated gear changing system in which gears correspond with given points marked on the lever mechanism. The system requires accurate adjustment of the front and rear derailleurs to work effectively.

L

Lugs Sleeves that correctly position two tubes together for the purpose of joining by soldering or glueing. Frequently decorative, lugs add strength by providing more surface area for the glue or solder to grip, and for distributing the stress on the frame.

P

Pawl Pin that engages a notch or notches in a ring.

Play (or excess play) Term used to describe looseness in a bearing assembly, characterized by clicking sounds.

Q

Quick-release clamp Used in place of a nut or bolt so that parts of the bike (wheels and saddle) can be easily removed.

R

Rear derailleur Rear transmission mechanism (generally cable-activated) that guides the chain up or down between the freewheel sprockets.

S

Stem Attaches the handlebars to the frame via the steering tube. The size of the stem determines the fore-and-aft position of the handlebars.

Spoke nipple Component on to which the end of a spoke threads, and which tensions the spoke against the wheel rim when tightened using a spoke key.

Straddle wire Short length of cable anchored to both brake arms of a centre-pull, or cantilever, brake. The cable passes through a straddle yoke to which the brake cable is attached. When the brake cable is pulled, force is distributed equally to each brake arm via the straddle wire.

T

TIG-welding A type of welding process in which metal tubes are heated until they melt and fuse together. The harmful effects of oxidization are prevented by tungsten inert gas being constantly directed at the join that is being welded.

Top tube The tube connecting the head tube to the seat tube. Usually horizontal on racing bikes, the top tube is often angled downwards on mountain bikes to give the rider more clearance.

Torque Any twisting force or power that causes rotation.

Tracking The alignment of front and rear bicycle wheels relative to each other.

Transmission A system that transmits power from the operator (human or mechanical) of a vehicle to the wheels to produce forward movement or drive.

Travel Term describing the extent of movement in a particular direction. The lateral (side-to-side) travel of the front and rear derailleurs is limited by travel-adjustment screws.

Treadle drive A system designed to drive a machine by means of a lever operated by foot. The foot movement is linear, rather than circular like pedalling.

W

Wheelbase Distance between the wheel axles on a bike, or where the tyres touch the ground. On conventional bicycles, wheelbase ranges from 96.5–111.7 cm (38–44 in). Also associated with wheelbase are trail (the distance a wheel axle follows behind the steering pivot point; the pivot point is where a line down the head tube intersects the ground) and rake (the offset of the axle or fork end from the steering pivot line). Increasing rake decreases trail. Less trail gives more sensitive handling. More trail gives less responsive steering, but greater stability.

MEASUREMENTS
Cycling convention dictates that mountain bikes are measured imperially, road and touring bikes metrically. Exceptions to this rule include the cranks, which are always measured in millimetres, even on normally imperial mountain bikes.

Index

Index continued

ACKNOWLEDGMENTS

Dorling Kindersley would like to thank: James Walters at Covent Garden Cycles; F. W. Evans at The Cut, Waterloo; Richard Bucknall and Victoria Gibbs (Jane Stockman's photographic assistants); Simone Dearing for design assistance; Mike Grimmer for transporting props; Lol Henderson for hand modelling; and Peter Moloney for the index.

Picture Credits: (Key: *l* – left, *r* – right, *t* – top, *b* – bottom, *c* – centre)
All commissioned photography by Philip Gatward except for the following by Jane Stockman: p.20 *r* (all), p.21 *tl*, *bl*, p.22 Anatomy (all), p.23 (all except *tr*), pp.24–25 (all except *cb*, *br*), p.27 *cb* , p.28 *cr*, p.29 *tl*, pp.30–31 (all except *br*), p.33 *tr*, p.38 *cr*, p.39 *tr*, *tl*, p.41 *tl*, p.43 *tr*, *tl*, p.44 *tr*, p.45 *br* (both images), pp.46–47 (all except *br*), pp.48–49 (all), pp.50–51 (all except *br*), p.52 *tr*, *c*, p.53 *bl*, p.54 *tr*, *bl*, p.55 *tr*, p.57 *t*, p.58 *r*, *l*, p.59 *r*, *l*, p.62 Anatomy (all), p.63 *cb*, *br*, p.64 Anatomy (all), p.65 (all except *tl*), p.67 *cb*, p.69 *tr*, *br*, p.70 *br*, p.71 *tr*, *tl*, pp.72–73 (all), p.74 *br*, pp.78–79 (all except p.78 *b* and p.79 *b*), pp.80–81 (all except p.80 *b* and p.81 *b*), pp. 86–87 (all except *cb*), pp.90–96 (all).
Illustrations on p.24 *br*, *bl* by Janos Marfy.